Letter from Japan

Marie Kondo

with Marie Iida

Letter
from
Japan

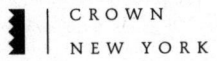

CROWN
NEW YORK

CROWN
An imprint of the Crown Publishing Group
A division of Penguin Random House LLC
1745 Broadway
New York, NY 10019
crownpublishing.com
penguinrandomhouse.com

This translation published in the United Kingdom by Leap,
an imprint of Bonnier Books UK, London.

Library of Congress Cataloging-in-Publication Data is on file with the publisher.

Hardcover ISBN 979-8-217-08808-9
International edition ISBN 979-8-217-08885-0
Ebook ISBN 979-8-217-08809-6

Editor: Madhulika Sikka
Assistant editor: Fariza Hawke
Production editor: Joyce Wong
Text designer: Andrea Lau
Production: Jessica Heim
Proofreader: Lorie Young
Publicist: Mary Moates
Marketer: Kimberly Lew

Manufactured in the United States of America

1st Printing

First Edition

The authorized representative in the EU for product safety and compliance is
Penguin Random House Ireland, Morrison Chambers, 32 Nassau Street,
Dublin D02 YH68, Ireland, https://eu-contact.penguin.ie.

To all who seek beauty in the everyday

Contents
章立て

Introduction
前書き

MORE THAN TEN years have passed since the English-language publication of my book, *The Life-Changing Magic of Tidying Up*. Since then, I've lived, worked, and even raised my children in the United States. I've also stepped inside innumerable homes across the country, where I helped people tidy their living spaces and answer that all-important question—*What sparks joy?* Looking back on this magical decade, I now realize the profound effect my experiences abroad have had on me. Now, although I am still active globally, I am currently based in Japan.

During tidying sessions and media interviews outside of my native country, I was never quite prepared for all the "Why?" questions that I would be asked. Practices that were second nature to me—greeting a home I was entering for the first time and expressing gratitude to things that I was letting go of—puzzled people. Their curiosity about my beliefs and habits challenged me. There were so many whys that I couldn't readily answer and was never expected to answer before. Working outside of Japan soon became an immersive opportunity for self-reflection, making me aware of my own culture like never before.

My upbringing is fundamental to my chosen career and philosophy of life. In fact, I don't think my method, which helps people discover themselves through the act of tidying, could have developed in any other culture. Japanese society isn't always encouraging of self-expression. It sees virtue in leaving things unsaid, in reading between the lines, and it can demand conformity rather than individualism. But I also believe that Japanese people, residing in a country where living spaces are often limited and particularly vulnerable to natural disasters, have a unique appreciation for making things last and living in harmony with our environment rather than in conflict with it.

I wanted to write this book to explore my own roots, and the questions I received about the more esoteric aspects of Japanese culture that are tied to my tidying method. The six chapters in this book—Cherish, Perfect, Consider, Savor, Purify, and Harmonize—represent some of the guiding principles with which I lead my life. They also reveal the values that flow through the arts, rituals, and sensibilities of Japan. I've also included numerous hints and perspectives in each chapter that I felt may be especially helpful to counteract the global problems we face today.

I also consider this book a letter to my children. Through their experiences living abroad, my children have grown far more curious about the world. But wherever they may find themselves in the future, there are traditional wisdoms of Japan that I would love for them to keep close to their hearts.

Finally, this book is a way for me to give back: to my readers, clients, and all the complete strangers around the globe who opened their lives to me and inspired me to explore my own background and, yes, what sparks joy for me. In a world rife with conflicting ideas and information, I believe it is vital for us all to understand and organize what's inside our own minds and hearts. A harmonized world begins with each of us attaining harmony within ourselves. It is my hope that this *Letter from Japan* will help you on your journey toward internal peace and enlightenment.

Marie Kondo
Tokyo, May 23, 2025

CHAPTER 1

Cherish

愛でる

Kisetsu 季節

I was far from home in New York City. Amidst a day crammed with publicity events, my husband, Takumi, and I were speeding through the city in a cab, headed to yet another press interview. Feeling a bit worn out, I gazed out the window, the foreign cityscape blurring into a colorless haze. Suddenly, a cheerful burst of pale pink caught my eye. I would have recognized that familiar shade of pink anywhere.

"*Sakura!*" I exclaimed. Cherry blossoms!

Takumi looked up. "Wow!" he echoed, matching my enthusiasm. "You're right. *Sakura!*"

"Beautiful!" I breathed, marveling at the clusters of cherry blossom trees lining block after block. It felt like bumping into a long-lost friend. Joy flooded my heart, tinged with a bittersweet pang of homesickness. The blossom instantly transported me to the spring days of my childhood in Japan—picnicking with family beneath a pink canopy, walking to school on an April morning, surrounded by a flurry of dancing petals.

In the back of the cab, Takumi and I burst into cheers each time we glimpsed another *sakura* tree. We pulled out our phones and snapped photos as if we had encountered a celebrity, and bemoaned our inability to leap from the vehicle and bask beneath the pink storm. My colleague, sitting in the front seat, swiveled to face us.

"They're just cherry blossoms," he remarked, arching an eyebrow. "What's the big deal?"

I looked back at him, mouth agape. "Because they're cherry blossoms," I tried to say. "They're so beautiful. It lets you know it's really springtime . . ."

My colleague shrugged. He regarded me skeptically before turning away. His nonchalance threw me off balance for a moment, but it failed to diminish my enthusiasm. I got right back to ooh-ing and ahh-ing alongside my husband. I simply couldn't stop.

Spring

Every spring, meteorologists in Japan begin tracking the *sakura zensen*, the cherry blossom front, as the flowers bloom first in Okinawa, which contains over 160 islands and is best known for its white sand beaches in the southwest, and gradually progress northward to the mainland. The Japanese Meteorological Agency uses fifty-eight designated sample trees across the nation to predict when the blossoms will emerge in each region. In rural areas such as Yoshino in Nara Prefecture, cherry blossoms transform entire mountainsides into cascading pink spectacles, while in urban settings like Shibuya, bustling with people and traffic, you might stumble upon a solitary tree flowering in an unexpected nook or cranny.

The meteorologists aren't the only ones who busy themselves with predicting the first bloom. Like many Japanese people, when I see the buds of *sakura* starting to swell, I grow anxious, thinking, "Will it bloom tomorrow? Maybe the day after?"

When I notice the first cherry blossoms beginning to open in a sunny spot, I excitedly tell my family, "The season's starting!" Then I consult my schedule and the weather report to decide on the best day for a cherry blossom picnic.

Japanese supermarkets in springtime will put on cherry blossom fairs, their aisles overflowing with *sakura*-inspired sake, pastries, and traditional *wagashi* sweets embellished with the iconic blooms and flavored with their fragrant leaves. From powder pink to pearly white, the *sakura* motif graces everything from kimonos to household items. The trees also flourish on the grounds of Buddhist temples and Shinto shrines, alongside school campuses and river embankments. Some, like the weeping cherry tree Miharu Takizakura in Fukushima prefecture, have survived over a millennium and are nationally recognized as a natural monument.

And where would Japanese art be without cherry blossoms? The flurry of pink serves as a dramatic backdrop for countless anime and films, as well as classical theatrical arts like *noh*, performed in masks and costumes, and *kabuki*, heavily stylized performances. They inspire pop songs, adorn ukiyo-e prints and paintings, and feature prominently in literary titles.

The Japanese language itself offers a multitude of

expressions and terms to capture their blossoms' allure: *sakura-fubuki* for the way the petals fall from the tree like snowflakes; *hana-akari*, or "flower light," evoking the gentle glow of the blooms in darkness. The word *hanami*, which translates to "flower viewing" in English, hints at Japanese people's long-standing love affair with *sakura*.

The word *sakura* first appeared during the Nara Period (710–794) in the Manyoshu, Japan's oldest anthology of classical poetry. Back then, the imperial court favored the fragrant plum blossoms imported from China, but as Japan cultivated its own cultural identity, attention gradually shifted to native cherry blossoms. The bloom of *sakura* in the mountains historically coincided with rice planting season. Because of this, Japanese farmers long revered the *sakura* as divine harbingers of a bountiful harvest.

In 812, the Emperor Saga held the first imperial *sakura*-viewing party, or *hanami*, an elegant affair complete with poetry readings and musical and dance performances. Cherry blossoms, which typically last only about two weeks, capture both the lush vibrance and fleeting nature of life. It's moving to think that generations of Japanese people have celebrated the *sakura* at these events with the same emotions that stir within us today. The renowned courtier and poet Murasaki Shikibu captured the essence of the *hanami* in her classic work, *The Tale of Genji*, weaving romantic intrigues and power struggles against the backdrop of cherry blossoms. Through such imperial poetry and literature, *sakura* became firmly established as the quintessential symbol of Japanese spring.

For centuries, cherry blossom viewing remained an elite privilege until the shogun generals of the Edo Period decided to share their passion with the masses. In 1720, Yoshimune, the eighth Tokugawa shogun, initiated widespread cherry tree planting in what would become Japan's most popular viewing spots, including the Sumida River banks in Tokyo. This era also saw rapid development of cherry blossom varieties, which helped them to spread around the country. The Japanese public, united beneath the pink blossoms, helped to shape *hanami* into its modern form: a celebration of spring with elaborate food and drink and a beloved national pastime accessible to all.

The fact that we are still able to enjoy customs established so long ago makes me sincerely grateful for our rich history. Our affection for cherry blossoms has now crossed oceans, taking root in faraway countries. In places like the Tidal Basin in Washington, D.C., cherry trees gifted from Japan many years ago continue to bloom each spring. When I consider how our shared love for seasonal beauty transcends cultures, it fills me with the warmest joy.

Why do I love cherry blossoms so much? I can think of innumerable answers to this question. First, it's that pale, gentle pink of the petals. No other color in the world sparks so much warmth and brightness in my heart as "*sakura* pink." Every time I witness this soft hue in the spring air, my heart brims with hope and tenderness.

And above all, the beauty of falling cherry blossoms is incomparable. Even as I hope to watch this beauty for just a day longer, the petals fall carelessly in the flurry of wind. The truth that a life with an end is beautiful quietly pierces my heart. How many more years do I have left to watch these cherry blossoms? Awakening the same delicate sensibility that moved the poets of the imperial court is an effect of the *sakura*'s presence.

Perhaps what I love most about cherry blossoms is their ability to offer an occasion for reflection—a moment to deeply experience a season through a single entity. In Japanese, we call the act of adoring something *mederu* (愛でる), written with the *kanji* character for love.

Let us consider this concept of *mederu* as we explore the four seasons of Japan.

Summer

In Koto Ward, Tokyo, where I grew up, a grand fireworks festival was held every summer. That day was special. When I was little, my job was to go to the Arakawa riverside during the daytime to secure a spot. By evening, I would change into a *yukata* (an unlined robe, usually cotton) and join my family, sitting down on the picnic sheet that I had spread out in advance.

As the sky began to darken, a quiet excitement took over the riverside. Then, a grand firework bloomed across the night sky, accompanied by a resounding boom! What followed wasn't a simple evening of entertainment. At the start of each series of fireworks, the name of the artisan and the theme or features of their art was announced. The viewers sat in awe, looking up at the dazzling display and quietly appreciating the momentary art floating upon the dark sky.

For me, fireworks are a uniquely Japanese emotional experience that has been etched into my mind along with the heat of summer. That's why discovering that in some countries, fireworks aren't limited to summertime was such a shock, and this realization made me appreciate Japan's fireworks culture all the more.

The way fireworks are made in Japan is also unique and deeply traditional. While fireworks in the West tend to be cylindrical, Japanese fireworks are spherical. Japanese artisans, some of whom belong to families who have perfected the craft over generations, pack layer by layer of colors and patterns by hand. Each shell can take days or even weeks to be completed, and they explode with perfect three-dimensionality. This is why fireworks are beautiful no matter the angle you look at them. Even the sound of the explosions has a perfect dimensionality. Indeed, the sound of fireworks exploding in the summer night is more than just a sound; it becomes a vibration that resonates deep within the body, reverberating into every cell.

Summers in Japan are stiflingly hot and humid. As evening approaches, however, temperatures decrease, humidity dissipates, and a subtle, sweet aroma emanates from the earth. I can still recall how special it felt to slip my arms through the crisp, cool fabric of a *yukata* in preparation for the annual summer festival in my neighborhood. Now, I only need to close my eyes to conjure the taste of ice-cold ramune soda, popular at such events. It's a fruity carbonated drink sold in a glass Codd-neck bottle, a nineteenth-century design with a chamber that holds a marble and rubber washer sealant to withstand the pressure of the gas. The marble is pushed into the bottle to open it. I also visualize the fireworks erupting in brilliant hues and patterns against the night sky, and feel the multidimensional sound resonating through my body.

> "Perhaps what I love most about cherry blossoms is their ability to offer an occasion for reflection—a moment to deeply experience a season through a single entity."

We might assume that joy is perpetually within our grasp in our modern world. After all, we incessantly scroll through images on our devices, curating our preferences and sharing our passions with the world. Yet, whether I'm working in Japan or the United States, one of the most frequent admissions I encounter while tidying with other people is that they don't know what joy feels like. Genuine joy—the kind that resonates deep within our hearts and souls—remains elusive.

When sharing my tidying method, I've always encouraged people to hold each item—hug it if necessary—to see if it brings joy. Going through this process of deciding what to keep and what to discard by touching each item hones our sensitivity. Admiring the changing seasons works in much the same way. Perhaps what we need to do more of today is to marvel at something that exists close to us, much closer than anything we can admire through a screen.

As I write this, Japan is still in the rainy season, humid with somber gray skies. Once the rain passes, it will be the height of summer. I've learned that contemporary firework displays in Japan now blend time-honored artisanship with cutting-edge innovation. The fireworks explode in time to music and drones are even employed to create dazzling, spatial art. While I personally favor the understated beauty of traditional fireworks, I know that whatever evolution fireworks undergo, they will be a brilliant occasional opportunity for us to lift our eyes from screens and look up together at the night sky, united with one another and nature, if only for a moment.

Autumn

If you've ever visited Japan, you've probably noticed that Japanese people are quite serious about food. The diversity, painstaking preparation, exquisite presentation, and almost fervent passion that accompanies each meal is truly remarkable. From convenience store treats to multi-course kaiseki experiences, culinary delights flourish year-round. But I think that autumn might be the most delectable season, living up to its reputation as nature's most bountiful harvest.

During my time in the U.S., the arrival of autumn would always intensify my longing for Japanese cuisine. Knowing how many autumnal delicacies are tied to specific regions and are only fleetingly available (and thus nearly impossible to procure from abroad) intensified my longing. But in my fourth autumn living in the U.S., while talking to my daughters, I realized something alarming. They weren't familiar with the concept of Japanese "autumn flavors." Nothing could be more serious! I immediately planned a trip back home to Kyoto in autumn, with its beautiful foliage. There we indulged in seasonal delicacies such as charcoal-grilled Pacific saury fish, served with a sprinkle of salt and a squeeze of lemon; the pine mushrooms known as matsutake in Japan; perfectly round, luminous dumplings specially crafted for viewing the full harvest moon . . . My daughters marveled at every bite. "This is autumn in Japan," I remember telling them proudly.

Japanese seasonal ingredients sourced from the wild are ephemeral treasures, typically available for a mere week or two. Their preparation often demands considerable time and effort. Take, for instance, the Japanese kuri chestnuts. Sweet and golden-yellow when boiled, they are harvested in autumn only after naturally falling to the forest floor, and their spiky outer shells make protective gloves a necessity. The outer shell and inner skin must be removed before the chestnuts can be washed and sorted. Every year, I look forward to making *kuri gohan*, or chestnut rice, for my family. The moment I lift the rice cooker lid never fails to spark joy—golden chestnuts emerge like hidden jewels amidst fluffy rice, releasing a savory, intoxicating aroma that permeates our home.

In our era of convenience, seasonality may seem less relevant to our daily existence. If we really wanted to, we could decorate our homes with sunflowers in midwinter and eat chestnuts at the height of summer. Today, I can't help but feel that nature and humanity live out increasingly separate timelines. When nature asserts itself, we may perceive it as an inconvenience or annoyance—an intrusion upon our carefully laid plans and schedules. But living alongside nature used to be a matter of survival. Humans needed to synchronize with their environment to ensure they had enough to eat and protect themselves from the elements.

In ancient Japan, people structured their years according to the *kyureki*, a lunisolar calendar. This hybrid timekeeping system, which considers both the phases of the moon and Earth's orbit around the sun, originated in China but was adapted in Japan to reflect the country's unique climate and natural phenomena. The *kyureki* divides the four seasons into six segments, creating twenty-four divisions called *sekki* (solar terms). The *sekki* is then divided further into three, resulting in seventy-two *ko* or micro-seasons. A *sekki* typically lasts about fifteen days while each *ko* spans roughly five days.

The twenty-four *sekki* begins with *Risshun* (Beginning of Spring) in early February, progressing through the equinoxes and solstices of spring, summer, autumn, and winter, before concluding with *Daikan* (Greater Cold) in late January. Meanwhile the seventy-two *ko* often bear poetic, descriptive names. Autumn's micro-seasons, for example, include "Rice Ripens," "Farmers Drain Fields," "Crickets Chirp Around the Door," and "Maple Leaves and Ivy Turn Yellow." These evocative names not only chronicle nature's gradual transitions but also offer gentle cues on how we might align our lives with these rhythms.

The *kyureki* was officially discontinued in 1873 when Japan adopted the Western Gregorian calendar as part of its broader modernization efforts. However, certain groups, including farmers, fishermen, poets, and artists, maintained their everyday rhythms according to the *kyureki*. I can understand why. The twenty-four *sekki*, each only lasting approximately fifteen days, give me a more nuanced lens through which to view each day, allowing me to "catch" each season in all its details. For example, on the day marked as "the time when insects sing," I once heard the bell crickets chirping in my yard and thought, "Wow, the calendar is truly alive." Today, guided by the words of the *kyureki* calendar, glancing outside and wondering what I might see that day has become a small daily pleasure.

Following the *kyureki* throughout the years, I've begun to realize that unlike other calendars that tell me of places I need to be and things I need to accomplish, the *kyureki* reminds me to slow down. It encourages me to pause, look around, and savor what nature has to offer. When I eat an autumnal food, I try to take each bite slowly and with a deep sense of gratitude. The delicious and unique flavors aren't the only gift of these delicacies; they embody the very energy of nature's cyclical rhythm at that precise moment. I don't want to miss it.

Winter

Winter draws my attention to the home more than usual. Few would be surprised to learn that Japan's year-end cleaning ritual is my favorite. As the New Year approaches, a palpable energy sweeps through Japan, urging its people to restore order and prepare their homes for the coming year. New Year embodies the concept of *fushime*—a pivotal turning point. The very utterance of this word encourages me to stand up tall and face the task at hand. *Osoji*, the year-end cleaning ritual, bears both a practical and symbolic meaning because it occurs at this critical juncture.

While Western cultures typically reserve major cleaning for spring, Japan's *Osoji* tradition has long been a winter custom. The practice evolved from *susubarai*, a soot-cleaning ritual at the imperial palace, which began in the Heian era (794–1185). This noble custom gradually spread to temples and shrines before taking root among the general populace in the Edo period (1603–1868). All the while, it maintained its spiritual significance as a purification ritual, performed to welcome the *Toshigami*, the god of the new year, who is believed to bestow good fortune upon a clean and orderly home.

During the annual *Osoji* I try to address each place I clean. While wiping the front door, I whisper, "May many blessings visit this home in the coming year." As I clean the grooves of the kitchen counter, I say with gratitude, "Thank you for helping me prepare delicious meals for my family." While dusting behind the headboard in the bedroom, I make a quiet wish: "May we sleep soundly and enjoy a healthy year ahead."

Of course, I couldn't complete my cleaning without the help of my family. My husband takes care of the bathroom, my daughters handle the hallways and stairs, and their little brother dances around to cheer everyone on.

Dividing the tasks this way during *Osoji* helps us deepen our appreciation for our home and strengthens our sense of family unity. These year-end rituals and customs bring Japanese people closer to the spiritual significance of our homes and the time we spend in them.

Just as life follows the cycle of seasons—emerging in spring, peaking in summer, ripening in autumn, and withering in winter—I've come to perceive a similar trajectory in inanimate objects. New possessions radiate a special energy, then enter a period of peak enjoyment—their "summer." Our relationship with them deepens over time until they complete their service. At the same time, there are items—like a well-loved book or a family heirloom—whose value grows with use, while others serve a purpose only for a limited time in our lives.

My awareness of an object's lifespan greatly influences how I tidy. Take, for instance, the first pair of sneakers my children wore. When I see the worn soles and dirt stains, I can suddenly hear their laughter as they dashed through the park that day. Still, once I see that the shoes have long been outgrown, I give them one final squeeze and let go with a heartfelt "Thank you."

Orime tadashii, literally translating to "folds that are

properly aligned," describes someone who conducts themselves with propriety and mindfulness. I believe this expression uniquely reflects a culture where garments were traditionally folded into *tansu* dressers rather than hung up in closets. The kimono retains its graceful form because it is meticulously folded and cared for before it is stored. I aspire to conclude each season with the same care and intention that I invested in experiencing it.

* * *

Spring, summer, autumn, and winter . . . to have something to appreciate in each season is truly a blessing. However, in recent years, the reliable seasonal indicators we have long depended on have begun to shift due to global climate change.

I've heard that it's becoming more difficult to predict the northward path of the cherry blossom front across Japan, and in some years, the summer lingers for so long that autumn seems to pass us by almost unnoticed. The cost we may end up paying for losing the subtle transitions of the seasons will no doubt be immeasurable.

Even so, I want to continue cherishing the fleeting beauty of nature that can only be felt in this very moment, no matter the circumstances. I want to value the time-honored traditions and sensibilities that have been passed down through generations.

What kinds of seasonal changes do you see in the place where you live?

What seasonal delights do you find yourself wanting to hold dear or *mederu*?

Just asking yourself these questions might make the time passing before your eyes look a little different. Becoming more aware of the changing seasons can help us realize how precious the present moment truly is. And that, in turn, can fill today—this very day—with sparks of joy and wonder.

Kawaii かわいい

On any given day, I must say the word *kawaii* five or six times, maybe more. It's undoubtedly one of the most frequently used words for many Japanese people. *Kawaii* translates to "cute" or "adorable" in English, but like "spark joy," it's a term that captures the inexpressible stirrings of our hearts. That feeling of warmth and comfort that rises from deep within us when we see something sweet. The soft pink paws of a kitten. A baby's pillowy cheeks. A dainty plate of strawberry shortcake. It's a feeling that makes us want to squeeze the object of our adoration and squeal with joy.

As a mother of three, I apply the word often when describing my children. My children are the center of my life, and when they make me laugh or do something fascinating, no other word can capture my affection with such immediacy. *Kawaii* regularly emerges in our daily conversations because of its remarkable versatility. When I encounter something that perfectly matches my taste—be it a piece of clothing or a furniture item in a style I adore—*kawaii* is the first word that spontaneously escapes my lips. For such a small word, it manages to say so much.

Kawaii is thought to have derived from the expression *kao hayushi* (顔映ゆし), which literally translates as "face aglow" or "blushed." First appearing in the late Heian period (794–1185), this expression referred not only to situations that were embarrassing and awkward but also to those that pulled at your heartstrings or evoked pity. As the expression evolved into the modern *kawaii*, its definition expanded to include the affection one feels for things that are small, weak, and deserving of protection. From the late Edo period (1603–1867), *kawaii* began to be used in the way we recognize today: a versatile term expressing affection, approval, and delight in all the things that make our world a little better.

Of course, no discussion of *kawaii*'s origins would be complete without mentioning the adorable illustrated characters that made Japan into a global *kawaii* mecca. No other country in the world is quite as dedicated to all creatures cuddly and endearing. This national obsession offers a unique window into the Japanese psyche. From Hello Kitty to Pokémon to Gudetama, fans of *kawaii* culture have at least one fictional character whose illustration makes its way onto their personal belongings.

My current favorite is Chiikawa, the protagonist of an eponymous webcomic created by an illustrator known as Nagano. Chiikawa has become an internet sensation since its debut, which spawned comic books and an anime series following the many comforting adventures of Chiikawa and friends. A small, white, mouse-like creature with a big round head, tiny rounded ears, and perpetually blushing cheeks, Chiikawa embodies *kawaii* in its purest form. Even its name is an abbreviation of the Japanese expression *Nanka Chiisakute Kawaii Yatsu*, which translates to "a cute small thing." Chiikawa is timid, shy, and prone to tears, subtly echoing the original definition of *kawaii* as something pitiable. Even Chiikawa's backstory is *kawaii*. Chiikawa, despite its small stature, lives in a large house it won through a lottery. Shy and easily frightened by monsters, Chiikawa often cries but always tries to be brave and help its friends when needed. Chiikawa communicates using its own cute language, often saying "Yada" or "Iyada," which are playful, childlike ways of saying "no" in Japanese. From looks to personality, Chiikawa is completely *kawaii*.

I first learned about Chiikawa through my children. Chiikawa is a big hit among kids in Japan today. At first I didn't think much about it, but something changed when I started carrying around a small cosmetic pouch with an illustration of Chiikawa that a friend gave me. Opening my bag and seeing Chiikawa's disarming little smile was like a reminder to take a deep breath in the middle of a busy workday. It made me feel warm and relaxed, as if this tiny creature was cheering me on throughout the day. This is the special effect of a *kawaii* character.

Kawaii merchandising came into vogue in Japan as early as the Taisho period (1912–1926), largely due to Yumeji Takehisa, widely regarded as the godfather of *kawaii*. An innovative artist and graphic designer, Takehisa worked during a transformative period of modernization in Japan. The Taisho era witnessed a remarkable expansion of mass media, including newspapers and popular magazines, alongside the development of telephone and telegram communication. Society began to place greater emphasis on individualism and personal freedom, and the increasing influx of Western culture nurtured the flourishing of various art forms.

In 1914, Takehisa opened his shop, Minatoya Ezoshiten, in Tokyo, filling it with postcards, stationery sets, decorative *chiyogami* paper, and *yukata* featuring his own distinctive and lyrical designs. He was a pivotal figure in the Taisho Romanticism art movement, a creative approach that masterfully blended Western artistic motifs with traditional Japanese aesthetic sensibilities. Takehisa became known for his portrayals of women, whom he often drew as willowy figures with large, expressive eyes— figures equally comfortable whether attired in kimonos or dresses and skirts.

Takehisa's women were characterized by a touch of melancholy that hinted at their rich inner lives. These representations captivated young women during an era when an increasing number of them were gaining access to secondary education and experiencing newfound leisure time and disposable income. By designing and marketing products specifically tailored to the sensibilities of these emerging modern women, Takehisa effectively spearheaded the *kawaii* movement, establishing a template for aesthetic and commercial appeal that would resonate for generations to come. By the way, the Takehisa Yumeji Museum in Bunkyo Ward, Tokyo, is one of my favorite places. The antique-style architecture and the quiet atmosphere are a perfect backdrop for Takehisa works, making me feel as if I've slipped back in time. It's very relaxing, and I like to visit the museum and the adjoining café.

Another key figure in the history of *kawaii* was the illustrator and designer Rune Naito, who made his mark in the postwar era when Japan was eagerly beginning its ascent into an economic powerhouse. The direct influence of Rune's work is clearly visible in much of what we recognize as *kawaii*. Rune loved using cute animal motifs in his designs, and his "Rune Panda," inspired by an encounter with pandas at the London Zoo, gained massive popularity in the 1970s. Rune Panda featured a plush body, pink blushing cheeks, and rounded ears—characteristics that continue to echo through contemporary *kawaii* characters like Chiikawa.

Rune's illustrations of young women also played a crucial role in establishing the modern *kawaii* worldview. His iconic "Rune Girls," first published in the young women's lifestyle magazine *Junior Soleil*, embodied post-war optimism through their candy-colored fashion, bubbly expressions, and large, sparkling eyes that looked toward the future. Rune is also credited with transforming seemingly mundane motifs like flowers, fruits, and vegetables through the *kawaii* visual treatment.

During the 1950s, when the home was still predominantly considered a woman's domain, there emerged a renewed interest in women's lifestyles. Goods featuring Rune's designs and motifs brought the *kawaii* aesthetic directly into young women's homes, enriching their daily lives with color and brightness. Later, companies began drawing inspiration from Rune's approach to merchandising. Sanrio, founded in 1960, became a consumer goods giant by appealing to young people through cute designs and characters like Hello Kitty.

It's fascinating that *kawaii* culture began as an effort to introduce a small bit of delight and uplift into our daily lives. Our connection to our inner selves remains surprisingly tenuous, and it becomes easy to lose sight of what truly brings us joy. Perceiving something as *kawaii* helps us rediscover ourselves and listen more attentively to our hearts. What we find *kawaii* is often a reflection of our inner selves—our choices reflect our unique values and tastes, and we experience a particular joy when we share an appreciation for something adorable with others. Nothing bonds two people together quite like their mutual love for something they find *kawaii*. This is undoubtedly one of the reasons *kawaii* culture has become such a global phenomenon. Whatever we find *kawaii*, it has a unique power to unite people from all walks of life.

I've already mentioned my fondness for the character Chiikawa, but what else do I find *kawaii*? My favorite teapot. It comes with a lid featuring a small bird motif. While it may appear simple to others, the curved line of the bird's back and its sweetly rounded shape can only be described as *kawaii* to me. Similarly, carefully folded clothes are utterly endearing in my eyes. Clothes that have been lovingly folded and stored seem to possess a sense of pride, as if their self-worth has been restored. The orderly rows of beautifully folded clothes standing upright in a drawer represent another delightful manifestation of *kawaii*.

If you were to visit my home, one of the first things you would encounter in the entrance is a small aquarium tank. Inside, tropical fish like neon tetras swim alongside tiny freshwater shrimp known officially as Neocaridina davidi. Shrimp aren't often considered cute. They have beady eyes and a hard exoskeleton that make them seem more alien than adorable. Their sharp features and bug-like appearance don't fit the soft, round characteristics we associate with cuteness.

So what makes these shrimp so adorable to me? Their antennae! When viewed from the front, these shrimp have precisely two antennae extending from their bodies, and their movements in the water—quick, little up-and-down maneuvers—are so charming. What one person finds irresistibly cute might not hold the same charm for someone else. *Kawaii* is a matter of personal taste based on your unique perspective. I'm equally fond of medaka, sometimes called Japanese rice fish. While more plain looking than their flashy tropical tank mates, the medaka, with their creamy-white color and comically oversized eyes, are quintessentially *kawaii*. I love watching their tiny fins

> "The presence of something kawaii can have a soothing effect on social interactions, and the shared experience of kawaii provides a community with a sense of unity."

flutter up and down. You can often find me in front of this tank, repeatedly murmuring "*kawaii*" to myself.

In Japan, opportunities to exclaim "*kawaii!*" abound at every turn. Cute and adorable things are everywhere. In shopping malls and local convenience stores, shelves practically overflow with *kawaii* items. Entire museums, cafés, and even streets are dedicated to the vast collection of *kawaii* characters created in Japan. When you next find yourself in Tokyo, try walking through the streets and counting how many *kawaii* things you can spot! It seems that an advertisement or storefront in Japan isn't complete without some form of a cute mascot. Even signs for hospitals and gas stations, safety warnings on elevators and subway doors come adorned with endearing illustrations of anthropomorphized animals or other inanimate objects. This ubiquitous trend prompted me to contemplate the deeper function of the *kawaii* aesthetic in Japanese society.

In recent years, I've observed that more tourists are venturing far beyond Tokyo to explore Japan's countryside. No matter which prefecture you visit, stopping by a souvenir shop before boarding the bullet train guarantees an encounter with a *kawaii* mascot you won't see anywhere else. In Ehime prefecture, you'll meet

Mikyan, a hybrid orange and dog creature representing the region's delicious satsuma oranges. Hikone City in Shiga Prefecture introduces Hikonyan, a white cat merrily wearing the blood-red samurai helmet with gold horns once donned by Ii Naomasa, a daimyo who ruled the region during the Edo period. Then there's Kumamon, a black bear with red cheeks and thin white eyebrows perched above wide, staring eyes, who represents Kumamoto prefecture. With his cheeky personality, Kumamon managed to become a national icon, generating a remarkable $714 million economic impact for the prefecture shortly after his launch.

While the trend began in the 1980s, today every prefecture and even smaller municipalities have developed their own characters. They are known collectively as *yuru-chara*, a combination of the words "character" and *yurui*, meaning loose, laid-back, and gentle. These mascots are far more than winsome figureheads; they are a clever marketing tool and cultural symbol that generate significant economic benefits for their respective regions. Functioning as working ambassadors, they represent local specialties, from foods to historical landmarks.

Whether living, inanimate, or fictional, these ambassadors

play a significant role in Japanese branding and advertising. Companies frequently employ 2D characters as messengers to communicate with their audience and consumers. Why is this approach so common? Perhaps the answer lies in Japan's historical media culture, where manga and anime have been prominent. It's possible that Japanese people have long been conditioned to find fictional characters relatable and appreciate the efficiency of visual storytelling. Alternatively, could the embrace of humanized inanimate objects be traced to the Shinto religion? This indigenous religion of Japan centers on the concept of *Yaoyorozu no Kami* (八百万の神) or "The Eight Million Gods," which posits that everything in the world—from mountains and rivers to everyday objects—is imbued with spiritual essence. I would be the first to admit that I see and interact with inanimate objects as more than mere things. The clothes I wear and the supplies I use in my home feel entirely lovable, as if they are protecting me and making my life possible every day. Perhaps such empathy makes me and other Japanese people particularly susceptible to the appeal of anthropomorphized objects with googly eyes.

Whatever the case may be, *kawaii* has become big

business. By incorporating playful designs and characters, brands can appeal to emotions, making products more relatable and engaging. This strategy works across industries, from fashion to tech, and has global appeal, helping companies attract trend-conscious consumers and even create viral moments.

A few years ago, driving into Tokyo from Narita airport after a trip abroad, I saw something remarkable. Jet-lagged and exhausted, I could barely keep my eyes open as I gazed out the window. The day was somber and overcast, with heavy traffic crawling along the road. As the cab inched forward, I started to recognize the familiar scenes of Tokyo: groups of high school students in uniforms, convenience stores, mothers cycling past with children in tow, colorful billboards and store signs. Suddenly, something caught my eye and made me sit up straight.

There were plastic rabbits on the road—yellow, smiling rabbits holding what looked to be pink flowers. A whole row of them, a barricade, lined the curb, standing next to a construction worker in a white helmet and a white-and-orange-striped safety vest. In stark contrast to the cheerful bunnies, the construction worker looked rather glum as he directed traffic with a red baton. It was then that I realized the plastic rabbits were traffic cones, ingeniously refashioned to appear *kawaii*. Sure enough, a sizable hole in the pavement lay behind the rabbits, surrounded by more construction workers operating heavy machinery and equipment.

Whenever I start to wonder about *kawaii* culture in Japan, I remember the day I saw those traffic cones. There didn't seem to be any practical reason why the cones needed to be cute. The adorable, joyful bunnies weren't there to advertise anything. An ordinary set of traffic cones would have done the job just fine. So why the *kawaii* treatment?

I once had an opportunity to talk with a business associate of a major domestic food company when our conversation turned to *kawaii* culture. When I asked him why so many services and corporations in Japan rely on "cute" aesthetics, he explained that *kawaii* things may be a show of goodwill on the part of the communicator. It's a way to project an intention to do good in the world and show consideration for others' feelings. This perspective resonated deeply with me.

Construction work can be an inconvenience to many people on the road and is often visually unappealing.

The traffic cones shaped like bunnies could function as a subtle visual acknowledgment of this disruption. They appeal to the public for understanding and project a message that they are ultimately there to do good. The *kawaii* aesthetic can make difficult situations more tolerable.

I mentioned before that, like *tokimeki* or "spark joy," *kawaii* is a word that expresses a feeling of love beyond words. But while *tokimeki* might be experienced as an invigorating, powerful joy, *kawaii* is warmer and more ambiguous. The presence of something *kawaii* can have a soothing effect on social interactions, and the shared experience of *kawaii* provides a community with a sense of unity.

These days, *kawaii* seems to be known everywhere in the world, requiring hardly any translation. Nevertheless, I had an interesting experience that made me think more deeply about its definition. In the wake of my Netflix shows, I participated in numerous media appearances and interviews in the U.S. and beyond. During such encounters, people would sometimes comment on my petite stature. I didn't think much about this, as I've long considered my height to be a part of my character. But one day, a producer pulled me aside after a television segment taping. "I'm so sorry about what the interviewer said to you just then. It was rude," she said, looking embarrassed. "She shouldn't have called you *cute*."

At first, I was confused by her comment, but when I realized what she was referring to, I was surprised. I had always assumed that "cute" was the equivalent of *kawaii* in English. Most people in Japan would consider *kawaii* to be a compliment. However, I understood that "cute" can sometimes convey immaturity or a sense of being less than. I know that, depending on the situation, *kawaii* can also carry similar undertones. But compared to "cute," *kawaii*'s definition feels much broader and more nuanced to me.

If you pay close attention to the situations or things that Japanese people call *kawaii*, they might surprise you. *Kawaii* doesn't always mean that something is simply cute or appealing. *Kawaii* things have character. They are wonderfully quirky. You might find that there is nothing cute about, say, your middle-aged, perpetually grumpy boss. But if you were to one day discover that the same boss unexpectedly loves dogs and you witnessed him smiling warmly at a puppy he found, it would be perfectly acceptable in Japanese language to call him *kawaii*. That moment when someone shows an unexpected quirk or vulnerability, they have the potential to become *kawaii*. *Kawaii* things aren't perfect, but they are wholly themselves. It's not surprising, then, that in the 1990s, *kawaii* became synonymous with the Harajuku district of Tokyo. Known for its colorful, freewheeling, and maximalist fashion, Harajuku continues to welcome bold experimentation in personal style. The neighborhood represents the rebellious side of the *kawaii* aesthetic, one embraced by young people eager to carve out their own identity without societal boundaries or rules. Perhaps you've seen the music video of the Japanese singer Kyary Pamyu Pamyu for her global hit song, "PONPONPON." If there is a perfect human embodiment of Japan's *kawaii* culture centered in the Harajuku neighborhood, it would be Kyary.

In her video, Kyary appears wearing giant pink and yellow bows in her hair, jumping and dancing in a room overflowing with vibrantly colored toys, food boxes, clothes, dolls, and accessories that look as if they have all gone through a *kawaii* filter. Her choreographed dance and music are fun and upbeat, but there is also a whimsical kookiness to the visual elements in her video. Even her lyrics, the continuous loop of "pon, pon, pon," feel largely nonsensical. The video evokes the boundless energy and joy of a young woman alone in her room, filled to the brim with only the things that bring her joy. Inside the safe space of her room, Kyary seems to say, her imagination is free to take flight. Watching the video, it's no wonder that the creativity of Harajuku's *kawaii* culture captivated the world and became an inspiration for countless artists and pop stars. Today, the most fitting definition of *kawaii* seems to be unrestrained self-expression.

As we grow older, we all start to feel the weight of societal expectations. We try to fit ourselves into a box and conduct ourselves according to the rules set out for us. Japanese society in particular has a tendency to maintain order through strict codes of conduct and a sense of propriety. Being an adult in such a society, it can feel shameful to carry around something that is considered cute, which can be seen as immature or unserious. Perhaps this only further explains why the concept of *kawaii* is so important and necessary in Japan.

Kawaii items are everywhere if you pay attention to them, and I love how they help you see the people around you in a new light. The Hello Kitty cover on your colleague's phone. Your intimidating neighbor's unexpectedly adorable Shiba Inu dog. That fluffy, hamster-like character from Japan whose illustrations grace your partner's favorite coffee mug. *Kawaii* items may be small, but they teach us a surprisingly big lesson: to accept vulnerability and quirkiness not only in ourselves but in others.

Against the pressures and the expectations we feel in our everyday lives, *kawaii* things give us permission to take a moment to relax and enjoy the things that we love. They serve as a reminder to make space for the softer sides of ourselves and other people—our love of *kawaii* things is what makes each of us unique. Think about all the little things in life you find adorable, sweet, or cuddly. What do they tell you about yourself? What can they teach you about what you need in your life right now?

Oshi 推し

When most people first learn that I work as a professional tidying consultant, they assume I grew up in an impeccably organized, minimalist home. But I don't think they would ever imagine what my older brother's room looked like. For as long as I can remember, my brother has been obsessed with anime, manga, video games, and everything remotely connected to these cultures. He was particularly devoted to the voice actors who worked in anime. It's common for voice actors in Japan to have side careers as singers or performers, and my brother would trek to every concert or event whenever and wherever his favorite voice actors stepped out from behind their 2D avatars to appear in person.

My brother's passion never struck me as strange or unusual. It was simply a fact of life. In Japan, fans of anime, manga, and video games are everywhere, participating in official events, conventions, and social gatherings to enjoy everything their fandom has to offer. My indifference to the state of his room changed when I became a teenager and my own interest in tidying grew. I began to research tidying and organizing in earnest. I went to bookstores and libraries, devouring everything I could on the topic. I learned about the various organizational methods and tools offered by experts in the field and tried them out for myself. Back then, it bothered me that no matter how much I tidied, my house never seemed to stay tidy. In my manic quest to "finish" tidying, I would often get in trouble for throwing away things belonging to my family without permission.

There was an unspoken understanding in my family that my brother's room was off-limits when it came to tidying. His room was special, an entire world of his own. I will never forget what it looked like back then. Anime figurines in pristine condition covered the walls, and volumes of manga in every imaginable genre were packed neatly yet tightly in his bookcases, each a testament to the worlds he had lost himself in. When the books failed to fit in those cases, my brother would simply pile them up— much to my horror—on the floor, where they inevitably formed towers that nearly reached the ceiling. He also had DVDs, CDs, and souvenirs from every fan event he attended. His room was a veritable shrine to his fandom.

As far as I was concerned, the countless things in my brother's room were unnecessary obstructions standing in the way of the ultimate tidiness I yearned for. Every so often, I would peer through the crack in the door of his room, clutching a garbage bag in one hand. "Do you really need all this?" I would ask him. "Why don't you just give it away? You're not using it." My brother, however, was immune to my consistent pleas, advice, and warnings. No matter how much I badgered him about tidying, he would go about his quiet ways, happily immersed in his passions. What a formidable opponent he was!

My brother was, quite simply, an *otaku*—a unique Japanese term that generally describes someone deeply passionate about a particular fandom and possessing expert knowledge of their chosen subject. *Otaku* is often compared to the English words "geek" or "nerd." I can't remember a time when I didn't know the word *otaku*.

I suspect this had something to do with my brother, who, to this day, remains the self-proclaimed, quintessential *otaku* in my life.

Another important *otaku* in my life is one of my oldest and closest friends. Like my brother, she is an anime fanatic, but her obsession is more specific. My friend is entirely devoted to supporting a particular character in an anime series she loves. With an expert knowledge of the character's origin, backstory, and personality, my friend considers her object of passion no less real than the voice actors whose careers my brother follows. At first, I was surprised to learn that my friend had become such an ardent fan of a fictional character, but I soon realized that this type of fandom is quite common in Japan.

Japanese culture has devised clever ways for fans to bridge the gap between the world of fiction and the real world. Fans often take pilgrimages to real locations that inspired works of fiction they love. I was once amazed to hear that my friend traveled all the way to Tokyo to eat at a restaurant that had launched a collaboration campaign with her favorite anime. The restaurant created an exclusive collaboration menu inspired by the anime character. Ordering from this special menu allowed her to receive original merchandise related to the character—merchandise that was unavailable anywhere else. My friend made the trip on a bullet train from her home in Aichi Prefecture, more than 200 miles away, just so she could add that rare item to her already vast collection.

There is a curious word in Japanese that encapsulates such devotion shown by my friend: *oshikatsu*. In 2021, the term was even nominated for Japan's annual buzzword contest. *Oshikatsu* is a portmanteau of *oshi* (推し), meaning someone or something you support, and *katsu* (活), meaning "activity." In short, *oshikatsu* refers to the various activities fans engage in to support their object of passion. An *oshi* can refer to entertainers such as actors, pop idols, and YouTubers, but they can also be manga, anime, or other works of fiction, and even characters within these forms of art. Interestingly, even animals, food, and trains can be considered *oshis*. Anyone or anything can be an *oshi* if they inspire you to support them and spread the word about how wonderful they are. These days in Japan, *oshi* and *oshikatsu* seem to evoke a lighter, more casual image than the general intensity of the word *otaku*.

While *oshi* and *oshikatsu* are neologisms, the cultural practice of this kind of expression of fandom and support has deep roots in Japan's history. During the latter half of the 17th century, new urban cultures flourished in Edo, present-day Tokyo, where powerful and wealthy men often served as patrons of the arts, helping specific performers advance their careers. However, it was the collective passion of ordinary people that propelled *kabuki*—a classical Japanese theater known for its dramatic performances and vibrant costumes and makeup—into one of the biggest forms of entertainment at the time. During the Edo period, woodblock printing—previously produced in monochrome—began to feature spectacular colors. Woodblock prints not only depicted scenes from theatrical works, but also showed *kabuki* actors behind the scenes, portraying their lives outside the stage. As such "content" became widely distributed, the public's desire to consume and support the art form grew. Much of what we now recognize as *oshikatsu*—the symbiotic relationship between audience and performers—seems to have its foundations in this era.

According to a national survey conducted by the Japanese advertising and public relations firm Hakuhodo in 2023, one in three people in Japan acknowledge that they have an *oshi* in their lives. They also spend a remarkable

38.8 percent of their leisure time engaged in *oshikatsu* activities. The verb form of *oshi* is *osu* (推す), which means "to recommend something to others." Going beyond simply talking about or exchanging information about a shared *oshi*, Japanese fans are known to celebrate birthdays and other milestones of their *oshi* together. An *oshi* inspires fans to write fan fiction, create original items for one another,

> *"Fandom as a culture may be universal, but I believe that Japan is uniquely passionate about the pursuit of passion itself."*

and support the object of their passion in various ways. There are plenty of businesses and venues in Japan that are more than happy to provide both the reasons and the space for fans to gather, no matter how unofficial the event may be. What started as a community activity has evolved into a full-fledged social movement in Japan, with a real impact on the economy.

Reading about *oshi* and *oshikatsu* so far, you might have discovered that you, too, have an *oshi* in your life. I think it's safe to say that, these days, *oshi* culture has gone global. Words like *oshi* and *oshikatsu* have helped verbalize our common desire to admire something with the unique power to lift our spirits. Fandom as a culture may be universal, but I believe that Japan is uniquely passionate about the pursuit of passion itself.

I recently went to a stationery store in search of a new daily planner. Among the heaps of ordinary journals, calendars, and diaries, I found a "life planner" designed specifically for *oshikatsu*. While there was nothing extraordinary about its leather-bound surface, the planner promised to help "track the happy memories with your *oshi*." This handy item includes a monthly log to help you keep track of your highly active *oshikatsu* schedule. There was even an "event report" section to record your thoughts on every concert, media appearance, and sporting event that features your *oshi*. The report even has spaces for you to illustrate what your *oshi* was wearing during these events and write down any interactions you may have had with your *oshi*, as well as the specific gifts you presented to them. It doesn't matter what the object of your passion is—Japanese culture provides the means for you to be as organized and meticulous as you want in your fandom.

Having an *oshi* is a little different from simply appreciating the changing seasons or adoring your favorite stuffed animal plush toy. Traditionally, being a fan meant being a consumer—a largely passive activity. But thanks to social media and the diversification of *otaku* culture, *oshikatsu* has become much more creative and personalized. A study conducted by the Department of Psychology at Aichi Shukutoku University defined *oshikatsu* as an action you take to connect your inner world to things and people that exist in the outside world. An *oshi* can inspire you to come out of your shell, and encourage you to act upon and engage with the world in ways you may never have considered before.

From my years of working as a tidying consultant in Japan, I also know that many Japanese people struggle with self-identity. Understanding your values and who you are can be difficult in our modern world, which is full of both physical and mental clutter. So much of what we love reflects our passions, our senses of humor, and our worldviews. Declaring what you love to others is a simple yet powerful way to identify yourself.

Thanks to the nature of my work, I've had plenty of opportunities to gain a better insight into *oshikatsu*. Many of my clients have shared that they have an *oshi* in their lives, and some have even told me how *oshikatsu* has created complications when it comes to tidying. I remember one particular client, a young woman deeply in love with a certain Japanese actor. In her house, I discovered countless cardboard boxes filled with DVDs of the actor's entire filmography, CDs from his brief turn as a singer, an array of merchandise, and figurines, both big and small. All of it was stored in boxes and bags, as if it were hidden away. When I suggested that she take everything out and proudly display her collection around her apartment, she hesitated. She confessed that she wasn't ready to let the world know about her *oshikatsu*, and, therefore, felt uncomfortable putting her obsession on obvious display.

I learned from her that the style of *oshikatsu* is deeply personal. While it was clear from the way she talked about the actor that she was a huge fan, she preferred to enjoy her fandom in private. Together, we came up with the idea of turning her sizable closet into her own secret *oshikatsu* nook. We dragged a bookcase into the closet and used it to display her collection of books, DVDs, and CDs just like in a store. We put up posters on the closet walls and arranged the figurines on shelves and in display cases. She was immensely satisfied, and I could see she looked a little relieved.

An *oshi* is meant to spark the utmost joy in your life, but it can also create a lot of physical items that need to be organized and stored. What's important is that all the *oshikatsu* items in your life are kept in a way that allows you to truly savor them. After all, an *oshi* is supposed to replenish your everyday life and give you the energy to conquer anything, not drag you down or overwhelm you.

Another client faced a different problem of having an *oshi* while living with someone else. He was a fanatic of *Sengoku busho*—the armored generals who fought during Japan's Sengoku era from the mid-15th century to the early 17th century. My client possessed not only an encyclopedic knowledge of the period, but also T-shirts, figurines, and posters of the generals who fought these battles. The only problem? His extensive collection did not spark joy for his wife. Understandably, she didn't care to look at images of bloody battles every day. "I like strong men," my client would say with a shrug.

The solution we eventually came up with was to split the couple's shared room in half. We installed a stylish wooden partition down the center, allowing both the husband and wife to enjoy their hobbies in peace. When something that sparks joy for you doesn't bring joy to the people you live with, it's important that each person has their own clearly defined space. No matter how much you love something, it's best not to push your values onto others. Each person's *oshi* is personal, and therefore worthy of respect.

Working with this client also reminded me of my brother and the time when his so-called mess used to bother me. I've since learned that when you're too troubled by what others are doing in their own spaces, it's time to take a second look at your own. Whenever I came back from seeing the mess in my brother's room, I often found my own closet in disarray or my bookcase overflowing. I realized that my brother's belongings weren't bothering anyone. He was happy in his room, deeply absorbed in his interests. Over time, I learned to do the same. I spent more time ensuring that my own room sparked as much joy as possible.

You might be wondering what became of my older brother. He's still a proud *otaku,* now working for a video game production company. These days, my brother and I acknowledge each other with mutual respect—and perhaps, even recognition. As overwhelmed as I once felt by his obsession with video games and anime, I now know that my own passion for tidying burned just as brightly. Who knew that in our family, there were always two *otakus*? My brother and I both feel fortunate to have discovered what we love at an early age and turned it into careers we enjoy. I often call myself a "tidying freak," but I know I could only have become a tidying *otaku* in a country like Japan. For that, I will always be grateful.

Mottainai もったいない

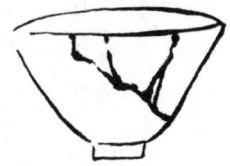

"Do you have any empty boxes?"

If you were to invite me into your home for a tidying session, there's a good chance I'd ask you this question. In fact, over the years, this has become one of my trademarks. Whether it's an empty shoebox or a tin that once held cookies, the KonMari Method encourages the use of boxes in organizing. They can divide up your sock drawers into tidy sections or keep together makeup products and stationery items that can easily go missing. I like to think that one of my superpowers in tidying is my ability to instantly visualize where a box might fit, no matter its shape or size. I'm a pro at tidying Tetris.

In Japan, the containers you receive from stores come

in a wide variety of colors, patterns, and sizes, often wrapped in beautiful paper, such as Japanese washi. These boxes are not only sturdy but also aesthetically pleasing, always enhancing the shopping experience. I could never bring myself to throw away such lovely boxes, so I've built quite the collection at home. I suspect many Japanese people share this sentiment, since I could always count on finding empty boxes in every house I tidied in Japan.

So, imagine my surprise when I started tidying in the U.S. and my request for an empty box was often met with a puzzled look. Of course, some of my American clients did manage to find boxes in their homes, but they were usually large, bulky cardboard boxes.

Another eye-opening experience regarding boxes came during one of my first holiday seasons abroad. At a Christmas party I attended, I was delighted to see so many beautifully wrapped gifts under the tree. My delight quickly turned to horror as the children began to open them. They eagerly tore into the gifts, with wrapping paper flying everywhere, shredding it to pieces. Even as a small child, I always unwrapped gifts slowly, careful not to tear the paper. I've always believed that wrapping paper could be reused—whether as lovely covers for books and notebooks or simply to wrap presents again next time.

While I had to admit there was something tempting about ripping into gifts with such abandon, a certain word echoed in my mind, keeping me from joining in: *mottainai.*

Mottainai (もったいない) is a Japanese term that expresses profound regret over discarding or wasting something that could still serve a purpose. While there are various theories about the origins of the word, most agree that it has deep roots in Buddhism. The word reflects Buddhist teachings that all things in this world are interconnected and that nothing should be taken for granted. When used colloquially, *mottainai* can evoke feelings of deep shame and guilt among Japanese people. I suspect this is because many Japanese people remember being scolded by their mothers during childhood with a cry of *"Mottainai!"* For example, when you fail to finish your dinner, hearing *"Mottainai"* means you've failed to show respect and appreciation for something, even something as small as a grain of rice.

While some speculate that the word *mottainai* has been in existence for over eight centuries, the philosophy associated with the term feels surprisingly modern. Perhaps this is why the word caught the attention of

Kenyan environmental activist and Nobel Peace Prize Laureate Wangarĩ Maathai in 2005. During her visit to Japan, Maathai asked her Japanese colleagues if there was an equivalent to the phrase "Reduce, Reuse, Recycle" in Japanese. They answered with *"Mottainai."* Maathai was impressed with how the word encapsulated the three foundational Rs of environmental conservation and added a fourth R: *Respect.* She understood that the spirit of *mottainai* encourages us to respect and appreciate Earth's limited resources. Maathai went on to spread the concept globally, using *mottainai* as a rallying cry for environmental protection when addressing the UN Commission on the Status of Women.

So how did such a culture of *mottainai* develop in Japan? Upon investigation, there seems to be a connection to the period when Japan maintained a long-standing policy of national isolation. From 1603 to 1868, Japan was under the military rule of the Tokugawa shogunate, which implemented an isolationist policy that restricted travel and trade. This meant that Japan had to operate within the constraints of its available resources, requiring its citizens to be highly efficient and avoid wastefulness. Because of this, Edo, the ancient city now known as Tokyo, flourished culturally as a sustainable, deeply ecological society for nearly two centuries. Through ingenuity, the values of *mottainai*, and a willingness to work with rather than against nature, the people of Edo maximized their resources and developed the skills necessary to sustain a population of one million—the largest city in the world at the time.

Today, we rely on advanced technology to make our society sustainable. The pre-industrial city of Edo, however, committed to never producing waste that could not be repurposed. When something broke or became tattered, it was repaired and reused until it could no longer serve any purpose. Historians credit the vast number of refurbishing and recycling businesses in Edo for creating "Edonomy"—an "efficient closed loop system where all waste was used to support production and previously produced items were repaired and reused."

When ordinary citizens of Edo found a hole or crack in their metal pots or kettles, they would rely on craftsmen who could melt down scrap metal to fix them. In modern-day Tokyo, a broken plastic umbrella would be discarded immediately, but in Edo, specialist repairmen would buy old umbrellas, disassemble the bamboo frames, and repair and resell them to new buyers. Used clothing dealers also spawned a huge industry in Edo. Tracking the life cycle of a single piece of kimono reveals how thorough the people of Edo were with their recycling. Since cotton was scarce, a garment would be used until it was well-worn. Then it would be washed and taken to a dealer to be exchanged for refurbished items or cut up into diapers or floor cloths. Finally, after exhausting its utility, the cloths would be burned, and the ash would be used as an additive in fertilizers to help grow more cotton.

> "Wabi-Sabi, the Japanese philosophy that finds beauty in imperfection, transience, and the natural aging process — could only have emerged from realizing that not a single thing in this world is eternal."

As the people of Edo carried out each step that contributed to the sustainability of their city, they honed their skills and crafts to the point where these activities became elevated to the level of art. So much beauty was generated through the continuous cycle of life that everyday items underwent. I had firsthand experience of this when I took a lesson in *kintsugi* for the first time.

I have a favorite plate with a rabbit motif that I like to use for breakfast every morning. When I accidentally cracked the edge of this plate, I was heartbroken—until I realized it was an opportunity to learn *kintsugi*. *Kintsugi* is the Japanese art of repairing broken pottery with lacquer mixed with precious metals such as gold and silver. The art form has been practiced even before the Edo period.

I was fortunate enough to take a lesson from a contemporary ceramic artist. From the start, his lesson challenged the way I thought about art and the concept of perfection. In class, he handed me a plate—not my rabbit plate, thank goodness—and instructed me to break it deliberately! I was stunned, but he insisted that it was possible to enjoy breaking something and then putting it back together so that it becomes even more beautiful than before. Once the plate broke, he told me to observe the fragments carefully.

"See these lines where the plate cracked?" he said. "Which part looks the most beautiful to you?" He asked me to look closely at the warped lines, the details of the fissures that appeared on the plate as a result of it breaking. Once you identify the most beautiful parts, you begin to enhance them further by shaving them down.

At first, I had no idea what he meant, but as I watched the masterful movements of his hands, I realized that he wasn't simply repairing broken pottery—he was creating something entirely new. Restoring something to its original form is not the point of *kintsugi*. It is the pursuit of beauty in the process of repairing that truly matters.

In our modern world, we often consider things that remain unchanged as perfect. We expect our homes, for instance, to remain sturdy and strong, staying the same no matter what comes our way. Yet in the past, Japanese homes were meant to change with the seasons. An aesthetic like *wabi-sabi*—the Japanese philosophy that finds beauty in imperfection, transience, and the natural aging process—could only have emerged from the sadness that comes with realizing that not a single thing in this world is fixed or eternal. Instead of despairing over this realization, how wonderful it is that the people of the past were able to find beauty in imperfection—things that break, become older, and wither.

Now, I'm gazing upon my favorite rabbit plate, which I have mended myself using the skill of *kintsugi*. Though the part that was fixed is very small, the plate has become a true original. Its visible marks of repair are reminders of both the plate's history and my own, and looking at them only deepens my love for the piece. None of this would have happened without the concept of *mottainai*. I try to incorporate other ways of repurposing and reusing things around me. When my clothes become frayed, I try to mend them as much as possible, and I use parasols that can be repaired by umbrella craftsmen when they break. A kitchen cloth that has become dirty through repeated use makes an excellent rag for wiping areas outside the home, like terraces and the exteriors of windows. I try to get every last bit of use out of it before throwing it away.

Of course, you might find it puzzling that someone who helps others identify what to let go of in their lives should also value the very sensibility that makes it so difficult for people to do so. Wouldn't the idea of *mottainai* become an obstacle to tidying? In fact, I've heard my clients utter the word often during our tidying sessions. Surrounded by things that no longer spark joy for them, they tell me—sometimes through tears—that they can't bring themselves to let go of anything because, yes, it's *mottainai*.

It was expensive. I never used it. Maybe I can still wear it. It's amazing how much shame and guilt something we've never used can conjure in us. When a client tells me they can't let go of something because it's *mottainai*, I always remind them that the feeling itself is natural and even wonderful. That guilt shows you value the things around you and want to take better care of them. *Mottainai* is such an intriguing word. As I mentioned, it's an expression of regret over waste. But the word is also about unmet potential and possibilities.

I sometimes ask myself: What do I consider most *mottainai*? Things that never spark joy, things that make us feel ambivalent or uneasy, lying dormant in our homes forever. Things that are never used because we fear they will change or break. Our physical environment becomes cluttered by things that hinder our ability to reach the fullest potential of our lives.

In the KonMari method of tidying, we learn to choose what sparks joy for us. But I feel that a lot of people forget that this is only half of the magic. The rest is about what you do—how you live—with the things that you decide to keep. Tidying teaches you to identify what you truly love, but it also changes how you live going forward. You shift into a life in which you take care of the things you have and create less waste. Things no longer overwhelm you because you are in better control of what you bring into your life.

CHAPTER 2

Perfect
極める

Chado 茶道

I attended an all-girls junior and senior high school in Tokyo, where many students engaged in extracurricular activities such as sports, theater, debating society, and band. My extracurricular? Of course, it was going straight home and researching the way of tidying! Well, that's what I'd like to say, but in reality I chose something a little different.

If I were to tell you that I chose to study Japanese tea ceremony as my extracurricular activity, you might assume that I was prim and proper from a young age. What imagery does the tea ceremony evoke? Perhaps an elegant woman dressed in a beautiful kimono. Or matcha, as brilliantly green as the leaves of summer, served in a ceramic vessel that nestles perfectly in your hands. You might imagine the perfect calm that washes over you as you take a sip, gazing up on the view of a stone garden beyond. I'm sorry to say that such sophistication was far from my adolescent mind when I joined the tea ceremony club. My motivation? It was sweets.

While I've never studied abroad, schools in Japan when I was growing up were probably much stricter than their equivalents in the West. I loved my school, but it had its fair share of rules and regulations. Eating outside of lunch hour, for example, was prohibited. Snacking at school was unthinkable. Given this context, you can probably imagine why I became interested when I heard that eating sweets was an essential part of the Japanese tea ceremony, known as *chado* (茶道). *Cha* (茶) means "tea" and *do* (道) is "way"—*chado* translates to "the way of tea."

A cornerstone of Japan's classical arts, the tea ceremony boasts a rich history spanning over eight centuries. Yet my understanding of this ritual back then was that it simply involved drinking tea and somewhere along the way sweets were also consumed. The idea of eating sweets at school felt extraordinary to me. And when you are a teenager, anything extraordinary or unconventional is irresistible. For me, learning *chado* felt much more thrilling than joining any other club. Little did I anticipate the profound impact this ancient practice would have on my life. The tea ceremony offered a form of extraordinariness that far surpassed my expectations.

Tea clubs are a staple in many Japanese high schools. Some schools even have dedicated tearooms, but since my school had none, our club activities took place in a multi-purpose room with *tatami*—traditional straw mat—flooring. I remember our instructor always burned some incense before our arrival. As we slid open the door, a crisp, peppery fragrance would welcome us inside. It served as a kind of transition, signaling to us that we were stepping into a realm distinct from our ordinary school life.

What I anticipated in my weekly *chado* club was simply brewing and sipping tea alongside my fellow members. But once our lessons began, I was shocked to learn how wrong I was.

"When you first step into the room, lead with your left foot," our teacher instructed on day one. "When you walk, remember that a single *tatami* mat should be crossed in six steps."

I glanced down, noting that a standard *tatami*

measures roughly three by six feet. Suddenly, I found myself adjusting my stride to cross in precisely six steps. Following this came the lessons on bowing, standing, and sitting.

We also had to remain in the *seiza* position the entire time we were sitting. Within ten minutes my legs would grow numb, and when I stood up I was as shaky as a baby deer. It was far from the refined teatime I had imagined. It also seemed an awfully long time before we'd actually *prepare* tea, let alone drink it. Mercifully, we were afforded the chance to savor the prepared tea with a sweet snack every week. In this regard, the *chado* club kept its promise.

The way of tea is paved with rules. I was corrected on everything from the way I placed my hand against a tea bowl to my technique for ladling water from the iron kettle. The sheer volume and intricacy of these rules astounded me—they seemed to leave no wiggle room whatsoever. Initially, I felt some resistance to being put in such a tight box. After all, hadn't I joined this club to do something that was otherwise prohibited? Yet our teacher emphasized that only through diligent repetition could our bodies learn to move with grace and economy, achieving a kind of harmony that not only looked but felt beautiful.

Every week before practice, the members of the *chado* club would hang around, engaging in excited chitchat. We were high school girls, after all. Once our lessons began, however, a respectful silence would fall over us. We straightened our postures and carried out each movement with deliberate purpose, feeling a little more grown up in the process. We instinctively understood that a tea ceremony was something that we needed to *kiwameru* (極める), the Japanese word for achieving mastery or perfection. We also recognized that three short years of high school were not enough for true mastery; *chado* might require two or even three decades to master—an unfathomably long time in my high school mind.

In Japan, numerous schools of tea ceremony exist, each with its own distinctive approach. In our high school setting, we focused on the basics. During practice, students assumed different roles in the ceremony. Upperclassmen performed the *temae* (点前), the intricate sequence of steps for preparing and presenting tea, while the younger students began in the *mizuya* (*mizu* 水 meaning water, *ya* 屋 meaning dwelling)—a preparation area that acts like a kitchen adjacent to the tearoom. It was here that I first encountered the exquisite array of utensils used in the ceremony, each with its own specific name that must be memorized.

In a tea ceremony, matcha—finely powdered green tea leaves—is whisked with hot water and air in a bowl. This seemingly simple act comprises many steps, each imbued with profound significance. Before tea preparation begins, utensils must be ritually purified using a *fukusa*, a double-layered silk cloth meticulously folded and sewn. Whenever I participate in a tea ceremony, I always marvel at the grace with which a skilled host manipulates the *fukusa*. Typically suspended from a kimono's belt, the *fukusa* comes alive in expert hands. The host's fingers glide across the silk, deftly folding it into an inverted triangle. Then, grasping opposite corners, she stretches the cloth taut, producing a crisp "snap" in the tearoom's hushed atmosphere.

The matcha powder is kept in a tea caddy known as a *natsume*. The lustrous black lacquer on the lidded vessel creates an illusion of depth and weight, yet the *natsume* feels surprisingly light and delicate in your hands, like a small bird. At the start of the tea ceremony, the tea utensils, including the *natsume*, must be purified with the *fukusa* cloth. The ritual purification is performed in front of the guests who will be served the tea. I love watching the *fukusa* glide gently over the *natsume*, cleaning and polishing the smooth surfaces in precise order.

Another essential utensil in a tea ceremony is the *chasen*, or tea whisk. Carved from a single piece of bamboo, the *chasen* features delicate tines that curve inward like a flower bud just starting to bloom. The art lies in whisking with the *chasen* inside the tea bowl—vigorous yet without too much pressure. At a certain point, the host will raise the *chasen* straight up from the bowl to inspect it, making sure the thin tines remain intact.

> *"The simple act of drinking tea can become a tool for self-discovery."*

It's no secret that matcha is popular around the world. It appears in cakes, pastries, chocolates, candies, and a myriad of drinks. In a Japanese tea ceremony, however, matcha is used with simple reverence. At no other time does matcha powder look as vibrantly green, like something from an artist's palette. Tea can be prepared in one of two ways: thick (濃茶, *koicha*) or thin

(薄茶, *usucha*). *Koicha*, which mixes a larger amount of powder with hot water, requires higher-quality tea leaves and results in a dense, slightly viscous tea that demands more skill to prepare. *Usucha*, in contrast, is light and frothy and is the type of tea new students first learn to prepare in a tearoom.

One of the challenges in mastering the tea ceremony is that just as you begin to grasp the terminology and the etiquette, the utensils and equipment change with the seasons. Seasonality is also expressed in other ways. A tearoom features a small alcove called the *tokonoma*, which displays a hanging scroll, and an arrangement of simple leaves and flowers called *chabana* or tea flowers. These displays reflect the season, theme, or other sentiments the host wishes to convey. The beautiful Japanese *wagashi* sweets that accompany green tea also vary with the season, mimicking the shape and colors of hydrangeas in the rainy summer or fiery red fallen leaves in autumn. Only diligent practice can teach you to interpret the subtle cues scattered around the tearoom.

With so much to remember and do during a tea ceremony, you must focus entirely on the present moment, regardless of what's happening in your life. A tearoom is like a microcosm, a single room detached from daily noise and connected only to nature and what is essential. Even as a young high school student, I found the meditative focus of the tea ceremony both comforting and profound. Every aspect of the ceremony has been refined by past tea masters who perfected the art over time. I felt the weight and significance of what I was learning.

Powdered green tea was first introduced to Japan by Zen master Myoan Eisai, who returned from his studies in China in 1191. Later, throughout the Muromachi Period, the culture of enjoying tea developed among the ruling warrior class, then evolved into a uniquely Japanese tea ceremony that emphasizes spirituality.

In the sixteenth century, another influential tea master, Takeno Joo, introduced *wabi-cha*, a tea ceremony style that highlighted simplicity and rustic charm. While *wabi* in Japanese often describes loneliness and the hardship of solitude, Takeno used this concept to reveal a spirituality that finds beauty in imperfection and fosters modesty and humility. A profound reverence for nature marked the aesthetic of Takeno's *wabi-cha*.

The tea master whose name became synonymous with *chado* was Takeno's disciple, Sen no Rikyu. Like his master, Rikyu believed that the true way of tea stood in stark contrast to the lavish tea ceremonies held in the vast reception rooms of military generals. To perfect the *wabi-cha* style of tea ceremony, Rikyu began defining the spaces where it should be held, leading to the creation of the *soan* (草庵) or "grass hut" teahouse. The Taian within the Myokian Temple in Kyoto, thought to be the only remaining teahouse designed by Rikyu, is a prime example.

The Taian teahouse's interior measures just two *tatami* mats and is enclosed by clay walls mixed with straw. It features small windows and a single entryway so low you must crouch to enter. Samurai warriors were also required to leave their *katana* at the entryway before entering. Drawing inspiration from mountain village homes, Rikyu's *soan* teahouses remain dim even during the day, with narrow, crooked wooden pillars that still bear their bark. Rikyu also preferred using utensils and equipment that reflected the imperfect, natural beauty of the *wabi* aesthetic. His tea bowls, often red or black hued to cast a subdued glow in the dim tearoom, had slightly distorted lines, while the bamboo flower vase he crafted himself had a large crack running through its length.

Whenever I participate in a tea ceremony, I reflect

on the Japanese word for mastery, *kiwameru* (極める). Written with the *kanji* character for "extreme" or "maximum," *kiwameru* signifies pushing something to its limits or reaching a pinnacle. I've often wondered why Japanese culture holds such a strong affinity for the idea of mastery and perfection. I also share this passion.

Throughout my life, I've always known that I wanted to dedicate my life to tidying. My interest in tidying began when I was five years old. I remember flipping through my mother's home and lifestyle magazines and being captivated by the world of cleaning tips and beautifully organized spaces. At fifteen, I read *The Art of Discarding*, a bestselling book in Japan at the time, and decided to research tidying more seriously. I devoured every book on the subject I could find. Having experienced the transformative power of tidying firsthand, I was convinced it could change lives. I believed then, as I do now, that mastering the art of tidying was my calling. At nineteen, I embarked on my career as a professional tidying consultant.

Even as I refined my tidying techniques, I didn't always understand what it meant to perfect something. As I often tell clients, I'm probably the only person in the world who has ever fainted from the stress of tidying. My obsession with discarding things I didn't like led me to discover the joy of keeping items that spark joy—a lightning rod of an idea that changed my approach to tidying. Starting a family and becoming a mother taught me the importance of compromise and self-compassion. The quest for perfection in tidying revealed so much about myself and helped shape who I am today.

When I worked abroad, I was often struck by how openly people communicated, defining themselves through the exchange of opinions and perspectives. It was inspiring to witness. Yet self-discovery can also occur through a deep connection with a single inanimate object. During a tea ceremony, you might gaze into a meticulously prepared bowl of green tea. While the bowl doesn't speak, the art of the tea ceremony, perfected through diligent practice, allows you to engage in a dialogue with yourself. The simple act of drinking tea can become a tool for self-discovery. Did you notice how the layer of foam on the tea broke into the shape of a crescent moon? What memories does the shape evoke? How does the bowl feel in your hands, and what might the host have intended by choosing it for today? Look outside the tearoom—

what seasonal details catch your eye that you might otherwise have missed?

I've had the privilege of meeting many people who strive for mastery. I've spoken with tea masters, artisans, musicians, professionals from various fields. It seems to me that what they've learned from their crafts often reveals fundamental truths about life, simple yet profound. For instance, through my years of studying tidying, I've discovered the importance of confronting yourself, trusting your sense of what sparks joy, and being grateful for the things that surround you while living in harmony with them.

As for my own way around the tea ceremony, since I've been out of practice for nearly two decades, I've forgotten the finer details of the procedures. Even so, the sensibility I acquired from my past lessons still lives within me. Whenever I had some time during my trips back home to Japan, I would sometimes visit a trusted instructor.

The tea ceremony may seem like a sequence of rigid steps, but with practice, you start to see that each action in *chado* has much to teach us about the importance of each moment we are alive and how to honor the time we share with others. Participating in a tea ceremony clears my mind and reconnects me with my roots, not only in Japan but also within my career. There's a Japanese proverb I hold dear: *Shoshin wasuru bekarazu* (初心忘るべからず), meaning "Never forget the beginner's mind." The proverb, attributed to the *noh* theater playwright Zeami Motokiyo, serves as a reminder that regardless of age or career stage, maintaining humility and an open heart allows you to keep growing and changing. The tea ceremony returns me to the mindset of that high school student who ventured into the world of *chado* all those years ago, reminding me of how much I still have to learn.

A client once told me, "You're like the Sen no Rikyu of tidying!" I was puzzled by this compliment at first. Lately, I've started to understand what she meant. Sen no Rikyu helped formalize the tea ceremony's steps, creating a structured sequence from the guests' arrival to their departure. His teachings remain the foundation of most tea ceremony schools in Japan. I can only hope that my tidying method can have a similar impact on the art of tidying. Like the tea ceremony, many classical Japanese arts focus on perfecting a simple daily act. But it isn't the result of that pursuit of perfection that matters. In high school, I was disheartened by how long it takes to master a skill. Now, that realization motivates me. To put yourself on a path toward perfection connects you with all the masters who came before and those who will follow. My journey of tidying continues.

Do 道

One of my biggest concerns when embarking on my life in the U.S. was the issue of toilets. I wondered, *Can I really live without a washlet?* Heated seats, bidet functions, the sound-masking flush button, automatic cleaning, deodorizing features . . . Japanese toilets are simply next level.

Japan's commitment to comfort extends to toilet paper. For example, there's a wonderfully soft brand of toilet paper I like called Oshiri Celeb, literally "Celebrity Butt" in Japan. Its texture? Pure luxury. Treating even your butt like a celebrity—now that's dedication. Even public restrooms in Japan are shockingly clean. For many first-time visitors from abroad, this might be the most surprising part of the country.

Another defining feature of life in Japan is the dependability of public transportation. Since I was in elementary school, I commuted by train. It took exactly twelve minutes from the time I left my front door to when I got on the train. Every morning, listening to the news program announce the time, I'd leave the house at the same precise moment and slip right onto the train as it glided into the station. This daily routine remained the same because train schedules were *almost never* disrupted. Even when there's a delay of just one minute, you'll hear a polite announcement saying, "We apologize for the inconvenience." Whenever I hear this after some time away, I know in my soul that I've returned to Japan. Every day, thousands of trains move with precision, seemingly effortlessly. But behind such a smooth surface is the ingenuity of the railway companies and the strong sense of responsibility of each station staff member. For me, these details of life in Japan reflect its cultural and social dedication to the idea of mastery. Once you begin to tune in, you can detect it everywhere. The meticulous attention to detail in the way bento boxes are arranged. The labels on bottles specially designed to slip off with satisfying ease. Exquisitely crafted food samples displayed in restaurant windows that could easily be mistaken for the real thing (these in fact have avid collectors!). At supermarket registers, you'll often encounter cashiers who will astonish you with their speed and care.

An ordinary scene from daily life in Japan becomes elevated to a realm of mastery before we even notice. Where does this cultural emphasis on mastery come from? One theory is the collective value placed on *omoiyari* (思いやり) or thoughtfulness, the desire for those around us to be comfortable. However, I think there's more to it than that.

As I mentioned in the section on *oshi*, I think there is real joy in the pursuit of perfection. As you strive to master something, your skill level naturally rises, and the sheer pleasure of it compels you to be even more devoted. This chain reaction can continue endlessly.

It's the same way with my tidying. I feel my passion grow when I'm folding my clothes or devising a storage solution to house every item that fits just so. When I focus my mind to its limit and reach a state of selflessness, there is a sensation in which every cell in my body overflows with joy.

Take something from your everyday life, something

you care about deeply, and practice it every day. Perfect your task to its limit, and soon you'll find that it becomes a path, or *michi* (道) in Japanese. This *kanji* character can also be read as *do*. The concept of *do* (道) in Japanese is deeply philosophical and often translated as "the way." It refers not just to a physical path, but to a method of living that instills discipline and aims for inner growth. In Japan, there are many artistic disciplines whose names end in *do* (道). At first glance, they may seem like mere skills to be mastered, but there is a shared spirituality that flows through them.

Let's begin with *shodo* (書道), the Japanese art of calligraphy often referred to as "the Way of Writing." I'll never forget the first time I saw a live performance by the acclaimed Japanese calligrapher Souun Takeda. I was stunned. Once he thrust a brush soaked in *sumi* ink to the center of the paper, he began to move it fluidly, as if the brush took on a life of its own. Before I knew it, the character 夢 (dream) had appeared on the blank sheet of paper. Having practiced calligraphy under the tutelage of his mother since he was five, his energy as a lifelong calligrapher seemed to transfer into the characters. The words he penned pulsed with life.

In Japanese elementary schools, calligraphy is a required subject, and it was one of my favorite classes. We always began the class by preparing the *sumi* ink. When all the students took a solid ink stick in their hands and began to slide—*swish, swish!*—the stick against the inkstone, the classroom would become enveloped in serenity. Hold the brush, saturate it with ink, and face the blank white paper. The sensation of our backs naturally straightening, our focus sharpening as we dedicated ourselves to writing the characters. Even now, I occasionally recall that tension within the quiet that I felt as a child.

You might wonder how the simple act of writing a character becomes "a way." In Japan, since ancient times, the act of writing characters has been valued for its ability to organize the mind and reflect one's spirit.

The origins of *shodo* can be traced to China. When the art of calligraphy was first transmitted to Japan along with Chinese characters, the emphasis was on faithfully learning Chinese calligraphic techniques. In Japan, calligraphy eventually evolved into new forms that matched the country's own language and sensibilities.

The *kana* characters born in Japan are characterized by soft curves and delicate rhythms, and they breathed new life into calligraphic expressions. For example, the word *kanji* (漢字), meaning Chinese character, is written as かんじ in *kana* form. The distinctive tone of *kana* characters can probably be felt from their soft impression.

In addition to the beauty of the characters themselves, an aesthetic consciousness began to grow in calligraphy, particularly the way space is utilized. The flowing movement of the brush, the way space or *ma* is constructed as if to give one a chance to take a moment to breathe—such sensibilities gradually transformed Japanese calligraphy from character practice into an art form that refines one's sensibility.

One event where this Japanese quality stands out is *kakizome*, which takes place at the start of the new year. This practice of writing one's resolutions or cherished words with a calligraphy brush is not only done to improve one's calligraphy but also as a ritual to set your intentions for the new year.

In my family, *kakizome* is an annual New Year tradition. Each person selects a character or a word that symbolizes their aspirations for that year, writes it with a brush across the paper, and after finishing, explains why they chose it and what it means to them.

For instance, one year I chose "広" (broad/wide). It was a year when I strongly wished to spread the KonMari Method to the world. Another year, I selected "育む" (nurture). I wanted to spend the year with a renewed focus not only on work but also on raising my children. The word also symbolized my desire to make more time to experience music and nature, to nurture my artistic sensibilities. There was also a year of "土台" (foundation). My ambition that year was to work on my physical fitness and re-examine my daily meals so that I could build a stronger foundation for my life. It was also the year I decided to relearn the fundamentals of English.

> "An ordinary scene from daily life in Japan becomes elevated to a realm of mastery, or perfection, before we even notice."

A single word can bring out what you truly value, where you are headed in life. Your sense of value and direction can also emerge from the word. *Kakizome* is an annual opportunity for self-reflection.

The calligrapher Souun Takeda had this to say about the spirituality of *shodo*: "Don't try to write well, but simply write with a heart full of gratitude and amazement at what you're doing."

His words reflect the idea that Japanese calligraphy isn't done to simply acquire a skill but to walk "the path" that values the heart of gratitude and joy. The time you spend holding the brush should be a time you spend with your purest self. Having such moments embedded into everyday life reflects an aspect of the Japanese cultural attitude toward mastery.

The concept of *do* imparts a strong influence in *budo* or martial arts and sports. For example, *kendo*, *judo*, *aikido*, and so on. While these all have competitive aspects, they place importance on self-mastery beyond mere winning and losing.

In *kendo*, as the phrase "beginning with a bow and ending with a bow" symbolizes, practice itself is connected to spiritual training. Before and after practice, students must always sit in the *seiza* position and quietly exchange bows. This moment is not only for showing respect to the opponent but also for collecting one's sense of self.

During *kendo* practice, the sharp blows of the bamboo swords echo throughout the *dojo*, and sometimes fierce shouts of battle fly back and forth. Yet once practice ends, the swords are placed neatly aligned, and protective gears such as masks and armors are carefully wiped clean. Even as they wipe sweat from their faces, no one would dare to treat their equipment carelessly. The gentle manner with which a sword is handled after rigorous practice brims with respect and sense of propriety.

This approach to martial arts is founded upon the values of Japanese *bushido*, or the way of the warrior. *Bushido* is not only a moral code that includes values such as courage, etiquette, and sincerity, but an outlook that inspires one to treat the things in your life with care and respect. This spirit is well-represented in the ways of the samurai, who never neglected the maintenance of their swords, which were considered their "souls."

The deep reverence for objects also connects to the KonMari Method. In my way of tidying, things are never discarded; they are let go with gratitude by saying "thank you." I feel more than ever that this respect toward objects is a value that flows through the foundation of Japanese culture.

For a long time, I had never experienced any martial arts, but while in college, a friend invited me to participate in an *aikido* trial class. *Aikido* is a martial art that involves accepting the force of your opponent and using its flow to apply techniques. The movements demonstrated by the instructor were something out of an anime. Even when an opponent grabbed his arm, he sensed the direction of the force, twisted his body fluidly, and evaded as if drawing a circle. When the opponent charged straight at him, he simply took a slight step to the side and used the momentum to spin his opponent around. Before I knew it, the instructor was standing behind his opponent.

"Don't try to defeat your opponent, first accept them. Be in harmony with them." These words by the instructor remain in my heart. As I earnestly tried to imitate the instructor's movements, I remember my breathing naturally deepened, my posture straightened, and I felt a sense of calmness settling in. *Aikido* was so much more than self-defense or sport; it was a time to align my inner self.

Similarly, *judo* is another "way" in which you learn to decipher the push-pull of forces between yourself and your opponent, a sport where skill acquisition happens alongside propriety and good manners. While it's a world-renowned sport, its spirituality remains distinctly Japanese.

What is common to all martial arts is the emphasis not on the strength to win, but rather the strength to discipline yourself and respect others. As in *shodo*, the goal of mastery isn't merely about raising your skill—it is deeply connected to your state of mind. This reflects a unique aesthetic sensibility.

Japanese culture has plenty of practices that encapsulate the spirit of mastery, even if they aren't officially called *dō*. Whether it's *kado* (the Way of Flowers) or *origata*, the art of gift wrapping, they all strive to cultivate a clear and open heart so that the easily overlooked differences and nuances of our lives may be felt deeply.

You don't need to belong to a specific school or tradition to cultivate such an approach to life. The spirit of mastery is reflected in one's attention to detail and the commitment to perfecting something you're passionate about.

The joy of mastery is universal. It might begin as a simple thing you like and enjoy. But as you spend more time devoting yourself to it, your hands move with more grace, creativity emerges, and your focus deepens. When you make the decision to perfect something, your life opens to a kind of meditative stillness and satisfaction. Your life deepens more than ever. Continue on with faith in your own joy and soon enough, a path will emerge.

Manga 漫画

WHEN MY HUSBAND, Takumi, and I first moved in together after we got married, he brought with him a single copy of his all-time favorite manga, *Slam Dunk*, a Japanese comic book. For those unfamiliar with it, *Slam Dunk* is a hugely popular sports manga that became a sensation in Japan during the 1990s. The story follows Hanamichi Sakuragi, a high school delinquent who joins the basketball team to impress a girl. Over time, Hanamichi matures and becomes a skilled player through his involvement with basketball and his teammates. It's a beloved manga that continues to captivate readers and fans around the globe, thanks to Takehiko Inoue's unmatched drawing style and detailed psychological portrayal.

Like so many others, my husband, Takumi, is a huge fan of *Slam Dunk*. At one point, he owned all thirty-one volumes of the series. But when we moved in together, he only had the last and final volume with him.

"Why did you keep only the last book?" I asked him. "What happened to the rest?"

Takumi stopped unpacking and looked back at me, suddenly serious.

"*Slam Dunk* is no ordinary manga. Once you start reading a page, you'll be overcome with the desire to read the entire series from beginning to end. You'll end up spending the whole day reading," he said. "But I realized that this final volume is enough for me now. Reading this book gives me as much energy as reading the complete series without spending all that time. Just looking at the cover sparks joy for me."

Before we decided to live together, Takumi had completed tidying his own space using the KonMari Method not just once, but twice. As a result, all his belongings fit into five cardboard boxes. This didn't exactly surprise me as Takumi had always been tidy, perhaps even more so than me. Still, giving up thirty volumes of his favorite manga must not have been easy.

I innocently asked him what he liked most about the series.

"Oh, let me start from the beginning!" he exclaimed.

I've since learned the hard way that my husband can talk for hours about *Slam Dunk* if you let him.

Takumi is far from the only person I know who has a story to tell about his favorite manga. "What's your favorite manga?" is an excellent icebreaker if you're hoping to get to know a Japanese person. The question is sure to spark nostalgic musings about their upbringing and stories of how a particular manga provided lifelong inspiration when they needed it most. When giving lessons on organizing books, I must be careful not to let clients casually grab their manga and start talking about it. Once they do, time can quickly slip away.

Some people might think that comic books and graphic novels are for children and young people, but in Japan, manga is a well-established culture in its own right. I don't think it's an exaggeration to say that Japanese people refer to manga throughout their lives. Growing up, we learn about history, science, literature, and the arts through manga. Manga even appears in instruction manuals and brochures. Everything from Peter Drucker's *Management* to Victor Hugo's *Les Misérables* has been adapted into manga, reaching new adult readers who might not have picked them up otherwise.

One reason manga has gained such a wide readership in Japan is due to the many manga magazines published during Japan's period of rapid economic growth from the late 1950s to the early 1970s. At its peak, *Shukan Shonen Jump*, one of the most famous and influential weekly manga magazines in Japan, is said to have had a print circulation of over five million. In a time before the internet, these magazines served as a reliable source of entertainment for the Japanese public. Even as the Japanese publishing market has been in gradual decline since its peak around 1996, manga, thanks to the growth of digital media, has maintained a steady market.

While touring the world after the publication of my books, I've always been surprised by how much the global audience loves manga. Walk into any Barnes & Noble today, and you'll find the manga section situated in the most prime real estate on the first floor. In most global cities, there are manga cafés with books fully translated into the local language, where readers can get lost in the illustrated pages for hours, just like they would in Tokyo. During book signings, I've been able to bond with readers over conversations about *Sailor Moon*, *Dragon Ball*, and yes, *Slam Dunk*.

True fans know that manga isn't just a two-dimensional art form. When we think of comic books, we imagine pictures contained within a square frame. But manga defies such constraints—it is a kinetic medium. The pictures move freely across frames, sometimes even across pages. The position of the speech bubble can change, with the font size and style morphing in every direction to convey the message.

I've always thought that manga has a powerful way of depicting strong emotions. Characters in manga cry often. Sweat pours down their faces, their eyes widen, and muscles and veins bulge. There's anger, regret, sadness, shame, and euphoria. When something sparks joy in them, there are literal stars in their eyes. I once heard that when manga artists are deeply connected to a dramatic scene they're drawing, the sound of their pen slashing across the paper can sound like music. The kaleidoscope of emotions we witness in manga is a testament to the craftsmanship manga artists have perfected over the years.

Characters in manga are often on a quest, striving

to attain the impossible. Maybe a character wishes to be the king of pirates or the most powerful ninja. They practice, compete, overcome challenges, and face setbacks to grow stronger and achieve mastery. They want to perfect a skill they love. The Japanese word *shugyo* (修行) is often translated as "austere training," and this is exactly what many manga characters engage in throughout their stories. Maybe it's basketball, martial arts, or even cooking. Whatever they are training for, they pour their souls into it. Perhaps this sheds light on why so many of us are compelled to read manga. It helps us reconnect to that pure sense of purpose in life.

> "So many of us are compelled to read manga. It helps us reconnect to that pure sense of purpose in life."

When I was in elementary school, I visited my father's childhood home in Miyazaki Prefecture, in the countryside of Japan. While exploring the storage shed, we discovered my father's old collection of manga. The bookshelf was lined with bestselling manga from the time when my father was young. Spanning genres from sports and slapstick to martial arts, each title offered a surprising insight into my father, whom I had always thought of as a rather reserved and serious person. I realized that he, too, was once a little boy entranced by the world of manga.

My father pulled a few books off the shelf, his eyes bright with nostalgia. He flipped through the pages and began chuckling to himself as if he were little again.

"Which manga means the most to you?" I asked him.

My father's expression grew serious, and he turned back to his bookshelf. After ten seconds or so, he selected the manga *Black Jack* by Osamu Tezuka from a shelf that easily contained around 200 books.

Osamu Tezuka, often referred to as the God of Manga, created the foundation of Japan's postwar manga culture. *Black Jack* is one of his most well-known masterpieces. The eponymous hero of the manga is a mysterious and brilliant surgeon, but *Black Jack* doesn't simply focus on the recovery of patients through medicine. The author himself has stated that *Black Jack* explores a physician's dilemmas, questioning whether a doctor's duty is always to prolong a patient's life through treatment, and whether such treatment can truly bring happiness to the patient. Set in the medical field, which constantly hovers between life and death, the manga's various stories illustrate the preciousness of life.

Many readers of *Black Jack* were inspired to pursue careers in medicine. My father, now a physician, read the manga when he was in high school. After my discovery at my father's home, I read *Black Jack* myself. The conversations we had about the manga allowed me to hear about his days as a medical student and deepen my understanding of his approach to his profession. For my father, *Black Jack* wasn't just entertainment; it served as a guide to his life of service.

In Japan, people often learn valuable life lessons from manga. Even I, who spent more time tidying up than reading manga as a child, can attest to this. Since both my older brother and younger sister loved manga, popular new releases were always found in our home. I would often pick up the manga they left scattered around the living room, shouting, "Stop cluttering!" But even then— and this is just between us—more than once or twice, my curiosity would get the better of me, and I'd start reading. Soon, it would be dinnertime before I knew it.

My fondness for manga has also extended to my professional life. When *The Life-Changing Magic of Tidying*

Up became a bestseller in Japan, many readers shared opinions of my book, along with before-and-after photos of their tidying journeys online. Among these conversations, a certain manga artist tweeted, "I wish this book were a manga. I'd like to draw it." This tweet caught the attention of my publisher. In the spring of 2015, the manga artist Yuko Uramoto and I met, alongside my editors, to turn *The Life-Changing Magic of Tidying Up* into an official manga.

I was thrilled to see how an incredible artist would transform the ideas in my book. I knew that manga would allow readers to quickly grasp the important points of my method and provide a case study that highlights new aspects of tidying they may not have noticed on their own. Most importantly, I wanted to communicate through manga the passion I have for my profession. Each home I visit serves as my training ground. Each client faces their own unique challenges with tidying, giving me opportunities to further hone my skills. How could I visually convey the seriousness, dedication, and technique with which I approach each tidying assignment? While tidying may not be as visually compelling as, say, basketball, I would argue that there is plenty of sweat, tears, and hard work involved.

During the production of the manga, I brought together six of my former clients for a roundtable discussion about their tidying experiences. They shared stories about how their lives changed after tidying with my method. Their experiences and voices added so much authenticity to the manga and ensured the creation of a relatable protagonist and plot. In the end, *The Life-Changing Manga of Tidying Up* became a fictional story about a young woman named Chiaki, who struggles with a cluttered apartment, overwork, and a lackluster love life. After an embarrassing encounter with a cute next-door neighbor, Chiaki resolves to tidy once and for all with the help of a professional tidying consultant named Marie Kondo, aka KonMari.

Yuko Uramoto drew me as a joyful, pixie-like character with my trademark straight hair and bangs, dressed in a white jacket and skirt—my go-to ensemble when visiting clients' homes in real life. Chiaki finds "Marie Kondo" disarming at first, but she soon discovers that she can be pretty stern when needed—you might call her a Japanese version of Mary Poppins. My character waves aside Chiaki's embarrassment and walks right into her messy apartment to begin the tidying lesson. She is quirky, whimsical, and, above all, passionate. Whenever my character delivers the key commandments of tidying to Chiaki, Uramoto uses big, bold letters for the dialogue and strong brushstrokes in the background to give the scene a sense of movement and drama. You can feel that my character believes wholeheartedly in the power of tidying and its ability to transform lives.

People often say that Japanese people are generally quiet and reluctant to express many emotions in public. While there may be some truth to this, if the stories created in a country reflect its people's passions, I would argue that the Japanese are, in fact, quite passionate. The concept of *Shukan Shonen Jump*, the popular weekly manga magazine I mentioned earlier, centers on friendship, effort, and victory. Open any manga in the magazine today, and you're sure to find scenes of characters laboring for years, whether by themselves or under a master or teacher. The heroes often utter variations of the phrase "I must get stronger." Sometimes the challenges prove too daunting and they give up, but eventually, they find their way back on the horse or pick up that baseball bat or pencil. The narrative trope of striving for perfection can move Japanese readers, both young and old, to tears.

Stories of perseverance are still loved by many readers today, but at the same time, a slightly different type of manga seems to be emerging. When I'm casually scrolling through my phone, I often see ads for stories where the protagonist is transferred into another world and starts out with special powers, quickly overcoming one challenge after another. This has become an established genre known as *isekai* (other-world stories), one of the major trends in manga and anime today.

What's behind these popular stories, I believe, is our exhaustion. Burnout, an unstable society without end, the reality that hard work doesn't always pay off—perhaps such sentiments have spread through society, especially among the younger generations. So today, instead of pursuing the ideals of perseverance, we want to be healed by protagonists who are already strong, a world that rewards us without effort. The world of manga offers a vivid reflection of our contemporary mood.

Of course, there are days when I feel daunted by challenges big and small, as we all do. When I'm in need of some inspiration, I'm fortunate to have my own manga close by. I turn to the story of Chiaki, the protagonist of my manga. She often becomes overwhelmed by the clutter in her apartment and sees no end to the mess, and often opts for the easy way out, like buying extra storage tools and boxes to hide her things. This is the moment when "Marie Kondo" speaks up.

"Storage! It's nothing but a cosmetic solution!" she says to Chiaki, hands firmly placed on her hips. "You must begin by discarding!"

No matter how many times I read this scene, it makes me giggle, just like any of my favorite manga from childhood. "Marie Kondo" in the manga looks so sure of herself as she proclaims these words to Chiaki. Chiaki, for her part, looks hesitant and scared, but she slowly gets back on her feet to tackle her mountain of clothes. By performing the joy check on each piece of clothing, Chiaki's sense of self reemerges from the clutter. This is a fictional scene in a manga, but it's also true to what I've witnessed with my clients so many times. It's the perfect reminder that the magic worth striving for in life doesn't happen in a day.

CHAPTER 3

Consider

気遣う

Onsen 温泉

In the middle of the night, you awake to the gentle sound of water lapping the rim of a wooden tub made of Japanese cypress. No one is around. It's cold, but you brace yourself and roll out of your futon, slide open the door, and step outside into the chilly air. Beneath the soft glow of the pale moon, white steam rises from the surface of the outdoor hot spring.

You disrobe and sink into the hot water in one swift motion. You glance up at the starlit sky; the ocean, somewhere below, announces its presence only through the sound of its waves. You feel as if you are melting into the dark calmness around you, unsure where nature ends and you begin.

Or perhaps you take this solitary bath at dawn. You float in the water as the sun rises, the bright red and orange light glimmering from the sky and reflecting off the surface around you. You become a part of the new day, a new world. You feel the rejuvenating effects of dawn with your entire being—you don't have a stitch of clothes on, after all!

You follow this sunbathing with a Japanese-style breakfast: a bowl of miso soup, steamed rice, pickled vegetables, and plates of grilled fish. Simple, balanced, yet delicious. After the meal, you might take another bath. There's no rush; your only responsibility is to enjoy the bath, which offers a different ambience depending on the time of day. This is the epitome of bliss.

Before I can say anything more about Japanese hot springs or *onsen*s, I have to mention that I simply love them. An *onsen* is a natural hot spring, rich in minerals, used for relaxation and therapeutic purposes. The water temperature is notably hot, as it is sourced from underground, geothermally heated springs. Accommodation at an *onsen* can range from intimate inns to larger resorts called ryokans. In Japan, *onsen* resorts are considered an easily accessible luxury, as they can be found in many places around the country at a wide range of prices.

Just the other day, I woke up in the morning, realized it was a holiday, and felt like going to the *onsen*. I talked it over with my husband, and together, we decided to do it. We immediately made a reservation, gathered up our kids, and spent a few hours going to Aso in Kumamoto Prefecture.

Spontaneous trips are hard to come by when you're a mom of three. But sometimes, when the timing is right, taking the leap can be rejuvenating for the whole family. Kumamoto Prefecture, where an active volcano called Mount Aso looms, has earned the nickname the "Land of Fire," with many picturesque *onsens* that take advantage of its natural geothermal energy. Only a few hours after I had the instinctual feeling to go to the *onsen* and decided to pause my busy schedule, I knew Takumi and I had made the right decision. Because once I checked into my room, changed, and dipped into the hot spring water, I felt both my mind and body relax, easing into the panoramic views of the mountains around me. *Onsens* have all that I desire in a good self-care ritual.

This is how I spend the day at an *onsen*. Check-in time

at an *onsen ryokan* is usually later in the day, around 3 p.m. Part of the pleasure of going to an *onsen* is enjoying the energy of the region in which it is located. So, I take plenty of time exploring the neighborhood around the *onsen*, eating lunch, shopping for local specialties, and taking in the cultural and natural attractions. Once I check in, I always have a tea break in my room. Then, it's time for the first dip in the *onsen*.

There are many styles of baths that you can enjoy at an *onsen*. A room with a private bath allows you to freely take a bath, at any time of day, by yourself. For tourists from overseas, public baths at an *onsen* might require a bit more courage at first. Public baths can either be indoors, outdoors, or a combination of the two, and are usually separated by gender. They do require that you be completely nude in the company of strangers, but rest assured that the atmosphere is always respectful and relaxed. Everyone is there to rest their minds and bodies and want others to do the same. Besides, a public bath also offers the most dynamic views of the surrounding natural environment, be it a tranquil lake, stunning mountains, or the wide sea. After my first bath, I love changing into a *yukata* robe. *Onsen ryokans* provide robes for you to wear, and this ritual lets me know I've stepped completely out of my normal daily routine.

You need to take a break after a long bath, so I usually like to nap, read a book, or just sit and relax with my family, catching up with one another in ways we usually can't. Most Japanese *onsen ryokans* offer either dinner or breakfast, or both, with your stay. Dinners are often served *kaiseki* style, a multicourse meal that emphasizes seasonal ingredients and presentation, giving you a chance to enjoy the local flavors. For many visitors, these elaborate meals are as important a draw as the baths themselves. I also love how *kaiseki* meals are served at an unhurried pace that lets you appreciate each dish.

In the evening, after taking a short break after dinner, it's time to prepare for bed, but not before taking one last bath in the quiet stillness of the night. You don't need to stay in for too long. But the key is to submerge yourself until the water reaches the base of your neck. Doing this will apply a pleasant water pressure on your whole body, improving blood flow, and you'll feel supple and relaxed. After this final soak, I always sleep soundly.

Although I believe my routine is quite typical, there is something I'm particular about when choosing an *onsen*:

I make sure the *ryokan* offers an *onsen* that flows directly from the natural source, which is called *gensen kakenagashi* (源泉かけ流し) in Japanese. Some *onsens* mix hot spring water with tap water, while others heat the water when the underground water temperature isn't hot enough. *Onsen* comes in many different styles, but I feel the directly sourced *onsens* offer the most energy.

There are an incredible number of *onsen ryokans* to choose from in Japan, but all of them share something in common: an *onsen* is a distinctively Japanese culture that reflects the country's highest ideals about hospitality. At an *onsen*, you will notice considerate gestures throughout the day that make you feel seen, valued, and cared for.

Upon arrival, there are complimentary trays of hot tea and sweets waiting for you in your room. The facilities are well-maintained and immaculately clean, no matter where you look. In the changing rooms of the public baths, amenities such as soaps, combs, and Q-tips are fully stocked. There's comfort in knowing that you don't need to bring many supplies from home when you go to an *onsen*; everything from toiletries to grooming essentials is already available. When you exit the public baths, there are water coolers that dispense crisp, cold water, along with several massage chairs should you require even more relaxation (you do). At night, the futons are laid out for you before you come back to your room after dinner.

All these conveniences are wonderful, but what makes an *onsen* special is that even as you appreciate other people's consideration for your well-being, you also get to pay it forward. A dip in a huge public bath with strangers wouldn't be relaxing or pleasant without mutual respect and a willingness to follow bathing etiquette. Being nude at an *onsen* isn't a big deal for Japanese people. After all, public bathhouses in Japan have been around for hundreds of years.

At an *onsen*, you are asked to leave your shoes in your room and change into slippers or *geta* sandals. You dress in the same *yukata* robe as everyone else. Before you get into the public bath, you must fully wash your body. Personal spaces are respected. In the bath, there's no splashing or talking too loudly. Phones aren't allowed— you can forget about taking that selfie! Everyone puts towels back in the hampers, and items in the changing rooms must be handled carefully and put away in their designated spots after use. Every single person— not only the people who work there—has to contribute to the serenity. An *onsen* is a communal experience in every sense.

Relaxation is the obvious goal when you go to an *onsen*, but a strange thing always happens when I'm staying in one: I feel a great surge of creative inspiration. I know I'm not the only one who feels this way, because although you'll be hard-pressed to find a gym at an *onsen ryokan*, you'll often find small libraries, art galleries, maybe even an in-house pottery studio. Perhaps all that hot water gets the creative juices flowing, or maybe it's being cocooned in nature that unlocks something inside of you. In fact, throughout history, many of the most renowned poets and writers in Japan have penned their masterpieces while staying at an *onsen*.

> "At an onsen, you will notice considerate gestures throughout the day that make you feel seen, valued, and cared for."

From the Meiji to the Showa era, literary giants such as Natsume Soseki, Osamu Dazai, and the Nobel Prize–winning Yasunari Kawabata would often embark on extended sojourns at an *onsen* (often paid for by their publishers!), writing what would go on to be their defining works. The great fame that such literature achieved also elevated the cultural importance of the *onsens* that served as the inspiration for the stories.

Since my arrival here, I had made it a part of my routine to take baths in the hot springs every day. While there was nothing in this town that compared favorably with Tokyo, the hot springs were worthy of praise.

The above is a quote from Natsume Soseki's *Botchan*, a beloved novel about a young, rebellious teacher who is dispatched to the countryside from Tokyo to teach at a local middle school. Soseki based the novel on his own experience teaching in Matsuyama, the capital city of Ehime Prefecture, and his frequent visits to Dogo Onsen. Dogo Onsen, now designated a National Important Cultural Property, is said to be the oldest *onsen* in Japan, with around 3,000 years of history. To this day, visitors can trace the indelible connection between the novelist and the *onsen* with rooms and decorative features dedicated in his honor.

For these literary figures, the *onsens* provided a quiet and secluded refuge away from urban distractions, where they could soothe their tired bodies and minds after days spent rigorously writing. An *onsen* has a distinctive sense of unreality that triggers the imagination, but back in the 19th and early 20th centuries, the difference between the city and the countryside was even more pronounced. The customs and ambience of the past era were still alive in the countryside, unlike the quickly modernizing landscapes of the cities. Writers transformed such remnants of the past into literary settings and motifs. The fact that some of Japan's most evocative stories and poems are woven into the scenes of so many *onsens* makes them all the more beautiful.

In my own career, I've also turned to *onsens* whenever I felt stuck or stagnant. Putting yourself in an environment that's different from your normal place of work helps unlock new ideas, and taking multiple short baths can do wonders to refresh the mind and body. I can think of no better place to do creative work or try to solve a difficult problem. Even the idea for our company, KonMari Media Inc., was born in Atami, one of the closest *onsen* resorts to Tokyo. After relaxing in an *onsen*, I remember brainstorming ideas with my husband and co-managers. We were trying to articulate our long-term goal as a company and threw around many phrases and keywords. We ultimately settled on the simple, unifying vision: *Organize the World*. More than ten years have passed since that trip, but this motto of our company remains the same.

During the earlier stages of my career, I relied on *onsens* to recharge when I was particularly busy or worn out. Even when I didn't have time, I'd still squeeze in a trip to the *onsen* whenever possible. When I lived in Tokyo, I'd go to *onsens* closest to the city, such as Hakone, Yugawara, or Atami, which are easily accessible by bullet train. If I was working in Osaka, I'd go to Arima Onsen. If I received a request to do a talk in an unfamiliar part of the countryside, I'd check the location on the map and determine the distance from the nearby *onsen* resort. I was such a fan that it was almost as if I were accepting work just so I could go to an *onsen*!

Onsens have always had a profound effect on my well-being. I feel thoroughly replenished afterward, a positive energy coursing through my body. I once learned by reading a book on feng shui that hot springs are considered the best place to enhance your luck. In feng shui, the earth's energy is divided into five elements or phases: wood, fire, earth, metal, and water. All of these elements are believed to be present in hot springs, and that is one reason people believe they have such a rejuvenating and cleansing effect.

Before the publication of my first book, *The Life-Changing Magic of Tidying Up*, I was adamant about trying everything to ensure that the book reached as many people as possible. I was confident that I had poured all my passion and learning into the book, but I knew a little luck is always involved when it comes to the success of a project. Looking for a way to boost my luck, I started going to *onsens* located in directions considered auspicious for my personal energy. I'm sure all writers endeavor to promote their books in creative ways, but I wonder how many of them decided bathing was the way to go, as I did. Whether or not this contributed to the outcome, I know that *onsens* saw me through a particularly anxious time in my life.

Bathing is one of the most essential parts of a Japanese person's daily routine. When I was living alone, I used to bathe every morning and night at home. It was unthinkable for me not to take a bath every day. Yet, I had to rethink my routine when I moved to the U.S., specifically California. I once told my English tutor that

I had to bathe at least once, sometimes twice, every day. She looked at me in disbelief. I knew what she was imagining: me in a bubble bath, one leg tossed lazily out of the tub, with a champagne glass at my fingertips and candles everywhere. While my bathing ritual at home is never as luxurious as she had probably assumed, I learned that taking a bath is a privilege in places where water is scarce. I had a hard lesson in conserving water when I used up all the available hot water drawing a bath during my overseas trips to Ireland and France. Since then, I've become more conscious about learning and respecting the bath culture of each place I visit.

My experiences abroad made me see that the plentiful water of an island nation like Japan and the customs associated with it are a rare privilege—one that I hope could be shared for as long as possible. I recommend a trip to an *onsen* wholeheartedly when visiting Japan. I'm often asked which resort I recommend, but I believe in choosing an *onsen* that fits your needs. For example, you might head to Noboribetsu, nestled in the magnificent nature of Hokkaido. Or how about Yufuin, with its mountain tranquility that fills the soul? And there's always Atami, where the sea and hot springs blend together. Each hot spring resort offers its own distinct form of healing.

An *onsen* is a place that allows you to be considerate of others and yourself. I'm confident that whatever you are looking for, you will find it in the soft embrace of the water.

Soji 掃除

As soon as we heard the bell chime signaling the end of class, my classmates and I would pick up our chairs and place them on top of our desks. Then, we would gather both the desks and chairs and carry them to the back of the classroom. This ritual marked the start of our daily cleanup, which was my favorite time of day in elementary school. After all these years, I can still remember the sound of desks being pushed and dragged across the floor, mingling with the excited chatter of my classmates, while dust rose into the air, sparkling in the warm afternoon sunlight.

Once all the desks and chairs were collected at one end of the classroom, the empty floor would stretch out before us. One group of students would start sweeping with brooms, while another group would rush to fetch rags and buckets of water. We would dip the rags into the cold water, wringing them as tightly as possible to squeeze out the excess. After folding the rags into neat little squares, we would place them on the floor beneath our hands, then bend over in a position resembling a downward dog in yoga. Afterward, we would take off running, sliding in a straight line across the floor with the rags still beneath our hands.

I remember kids competing to see who could slide across the floor the fastest. This daily rivalry could get quite intense, especially among the boys. Once every surface of the floor was polished to a shine, we would move the chairs and desks to the other side of the room. Then, we would repeat the process—sweeping and wiping—on the other half of the floor. After the entire classroom gleamed with our collective efforts, we would return the chairs and desks to their original positions. This was something we did every single day at school.

Each student would clean their assigned area every day for a week on a rotating basis. While some kids were responsible for tidying their own classrooms, others had duties in places like the science lab, music room, or home economics room. If a class had pets, such as chickens or rabbits, a student would also be tasked with cleaning out their pens. You would see us everywhere—hallways, staircases, with our little rags and brooms, talking, laughing, and cleaning.

I also remember that there was a special role called class leader or *nicchoku* (日直) back then. Every student took on the role on a rotating basis, and responsibilities included taking attendance in the morning, calling out commands at the start of the class, assisting the teacher with small tasks, and supporting the class in other ways. The job of cleaning the chalkboard also fell to the *nicchoku*. The class leader wiped down the chalkboard after every class and used a special vacuum to suck the chalk dust out of the chalkboard eraser. This might sound easy, but the machine would send chalk dust flying everywhere, and whoever operated it usually ended up covered from head to toe in chalk. The dust would also somehow find its way into your eyes and mouth, causing you to cough. These were the familiar scenes during our cleanup time.

It probably doesn't come as a surprise to anyone,

but there was nothing I loved more than these cleaning rituals at school. I was that little girl standing in front of the open supplies locker with her arms folded, deep in thought. I remember rearranging the brooms in the locker, lamenting the lack of S-hooks, and racking my brain for a better way to store the cleaning equipment we used every day. While not every student shared my intense love of cleaning, we all felt a sense of responsibility for maintaining our school. We spent the majority of our days there, using its facilities, so why not take good care of them? From cleaning our classrooms every day to taking off our shoes and changing into slippers at school to avoid tracking dirt inside (we even had a rule that we must take home the slippers every weekend to wash them!), we learned to respect and care for the spaces we were lucky enough to call our own.

On school outings and overnight trips, the concept of cleaning up after ourselves took on new significance. Sure, we enjoyed the cultural or academic experiences at the places we visited, but I always had the feeling that those were not the main focus of our excursions. While staying overnight at an inn with my classmates, we learned how to fold futons in half or thirds and neatly stack them in the morning. We also made sure to carry plenty of trash bags in our schoolbags so we could take any garbage home with us. Whether we visited the local zoo or traveled all the way to Kyoto, how we left the places we visited always mattered. My friends from overseas who have visited Japan often ask me why urban areas in Japan are so clean despite the apparent lack of trash cans. Perhaps this will finally solve that long-held mystery.

Even now, as an adult, I continue to care about the physical spaces I occupy. Before checking out of any hotel, I always do my best to ensure that I don't leave the bed or bathroom too disorganized. After I eat at a food court or a restaurant, I quickly push back the chairs and straighten out the table and return as many items as possible to their original spots. Of course, like anyone, I have moments when I'm too busy to tidy up thoroughly and have to leave the space with a little mess. I always feel guilty and embarrassed when this happens, so I try to avoid it as much as possible.

Another experience in my adult life that reminds me of my elementary school years is how we sort and dispose of trash in Japan. Anyone who has lived in Japan for a prolonged period knows that the country takes trash sorting and recycling very seriously. Each city or municipality has its own set of rules, but waste is typically divided into several categories, and you can only dispose of a specific type of trash on a designated day of the week. It's also not acceptable to leave trash out the night before collection. If you live in an apartment complex in Japan, you'll often see residents rushing out of their apartments early in the morning to make a mad dash to the trash disposal area with their trash. Space is limited in a city like Tokyo, so missing a collection day means another week of trash piling up with nowhere to go in your apartment.

> "From cleaning our classrooms every day to taking off our shoes and changing into slippers at school to avoid tracking dirt inside, we learned to respect and care for the spaces we were lucky enough to call our own."

I'm always surprised by how, for the most part, communities adhere to the many rules around trash disposal. On the collection day for paper goods, I often marvel at the sight of magazines and newspapers that residents have neatly stacked and bound with string. Some municipalities even require zippers on clothes to be removed and sorted with other metals. And what happens if you make the mistake of putting out the wrong type of trash on the wrong collection day? A sharp-eyed superintendent will likely fish it out, leave it in plain view, and attach a helpful note scolding you not to do it again!

When I started living abroad, I was quite surprised to learn that there were many professional cleaners. The American school my children attended didn't have cleaning time built into the daily schedule, but they had janitors who took care of cleaning and maintaining the school. Once, I started scrubbing down my table and carrying away my tray at a restaurant, and a waiter who saw me joked that I was taking away his job! This was a real culture gap for me, but it wasn't hard to see the value in such services. I appreciate professions dedicated to different aspects of cleaning and maintaining our spaces. Even though Japanese people might still feel hesitant about outsourcing cleaning, the idea is becoming more accepted nowadays. There is no right or wrong approach to daily cleaning—each of us should do what feels right for ourselves.

I must also admit that after years of living with rather

strict cleaning rules in Japan, I enjoyed the more relaxed approach I experienced abroad. But if there is one thing I would love to share with the world about my early education in cleaning, it's the value of imagination. Even if you're not actively cleaning yourself, it's important to use our imagination to appreciate the effort that goes into maintaining a space. We should all recognize that cleaning is a task that creates value for ourselves and others.

My Japanese elementary school taught me not to take for granted the spaces outside our homes that we share with others—schools, parks, even sidewalks. I think about this often nowadays. Behind our digital screens, it's easy to feel as though we live in isolated bubbles, letting the scope of what we consider our responsibility grow narrower. Yet, the world we live in needs our care more than ever. Learning to extend our sense of responsibility and consideration to our surroundings might be the first step we need to take today.

Paying attention to the various approaches to cleaning in the world also inspired me to take a closer look at my own culture. If you're a movie buff, you've probably heard of Studio Ghibli. People around the world adore the beautifully hand-drawn animated films from the acclaimed Japanese animation studio. In Ghibli films, humans go on amazing adventures and encounter creatures straight from the incredible imagination of the studio's filmmakers. I'm a big fan, too, but I've recently started noticing something interesting about Ghibli films: despite taking place in fantastical worlds, there are many down-to-earth scenes where protagonists engage in, you guessed it, cleaning!

Take, for instance, *Kiki's Delivery Service*, released in 1989 and directed by Hayao Miyazaki. The film follows Kiki, a young witch who, as part of a tradition, must leave home at the age of thirteen to live on her own and find her place in the world. It's a heartwarming tale of a young girl's growth and burgeoning independence. Kiki eventually moves to a coastal city, where she befriends a kindhearted bakery owner who offers Kiki a spare room in her attic as a place to stay. Kiki is delighted and sets out to make the room, which is quite dusty and old, livable.

We see Kiki open the attic window and let in some fresh air. She places the chairs from the room onto the little dining table, then brings up a big pail of water and a brush. Rolling up the sleeves of her dress and the hem of her skirt, she gets down on all fours and begins scrubbing the dust-covered floor. She smiles as she works, her eyes brimming with hope and determination. Beneath the shimmering layer of water, the floor begins to take on a new brightness. From this very room, Kiki is about to start a flying delivery service using her broomstick. The scenes of her cleaning symbolize her resolve as she embarks on this new chapter of her life.

Another classic in director Miyazaki's oeuvre is *My Neighbor Totoro*. A beloved story of childhood imagination and wonder, the film introduces us to Satsuki and Mei, young sisters who move to a big old house in the countryside with their father to be closer to their mother, who is hospitalized nearby. Their new home is surrounded by an ancient forest, and the girls excitedly declare that it must be haunted. Satsuki and Mei begin to encounter an array of magical creatures, including the huge and gentle Totoro, a kind of forest deity who comes to watch over the sisters. And how does *My Neighbor Totoro* begin? With scenes of cleaning the house, of course!

Miyazaki infuses so much joy into the opening scenes where Satsuki and Mei move into their new home. The sisters dash through the house, opening what seems like an endless number of doors and windows. Their raucous laughter is enough to scare away the little mythical creatures that inhabit the house unnoticed. But the sisters work just as hard as they play. Satsuki and Mei fill buckets of water from the well in their backyard, and Satsuki polishes the corridor exactly the way I did in elementary school—she literally zooms across the shot as she pushes the wet rag with her hands, her legs kicking out behind her. This scene, which never fails to make me smile, is proof that all Japanese children know how to wipe floors this way.

I believe Miyazaki uses scenes of cleaning in his films to signal an important transition. He seems to understand that cleaning is a conscious act that allows us to orient our surroundings and energy toward the future. We feel, along with the characters, that something new and exciting is on the horizon. Cleaning is a way to open yourself up to new possibilities.

For me, no other film captures the role of cleaning in society quite like Miyazaki's *Spirited Away* (2001). The story takes place in a mysterious, spiritual realm a young girl named Chihiro stumbles into after her parents are transformed into pigs. To save them and return to the real world, Chihiro takes a job at a bathhouse where spirits and deities, or *kami* in Japanese, come to wash their tired bodies and heal themselves.

Director Miyazaki himself has said that Chihiro is not like his usual protagonists. Compared to other female heroines like Kiki and Satsuki, Chihiro lacks confidence and courage. When we first meet her, she seems a little flimsy with a lazy way of looking out at the world. She is a typical ten-year-old girl, a product of our modern civilization, who comes off as sheltered and inexperienced.

Through the hard work Chihiro experiences at the bathhouse, she grows stronger. She jumps into a huge bathtub and learns to scrub it down with all the power her skinny arms and legs can muster. She helps clean a river spirit, made filthy by pollution and waste. Of course, she is motivated by a need to help her parents, but she also forms deep connections with the characters she meets. By learning to care for and consider things and beings outside of herself, Chihiro comes alive.

Miyazaki has said that with *Spirited Away*, he wanted to create a film about a young person whose dormant powers are awakened when she becomes a part of society. In addition to being a filmmaker, Miyazaki is a conservationist whose films often explore themes of environmentalism and the consequences of human impact on nature. The work of cleaning that Chihiro performs in the film is deeply symbolic. It leads her to an important realization: she has a role to play and a responsibility to the world around her.

In Japan, the practice of cleaning takes root from an early age, woven into the fabric of daily life. It's not simply a chore, but a lesson passed down through teachers—at school, at home, and even reflected in our stories and entertainment, such as Ghibli films. Cleaning is an act of care, a way of honoring both our surroundings and the people who share them with us.

There is a simple Japanese proverb that I hold dear to my heart: "A bird taking flight does not disturb the water." Today, this proverb resonates with greater urgency for me. It evokes the image of a bird taking flight, leaving the water clean and intact, with only the calm ripples to remind you that it had been there. If only we, too, could strive to live in, and depart from, this world we share with such grace.

Omotenashi おもてなし

"So, people are coming over to our house . . ." I mumbled this to my husband with a sigh.

Not long after I had moved to the United States from Japan, I was confronted by a reality that I rarely had to face back in my native country: I was going to have guests over to my home. It would have been one thing to host some close friends for a casual get-together, but the guests coming over were all from my professional network: agents and representatives of a publishing house I was working with at the time.

I became immediately self-conscious. *They're probably expecting a lot from you and your home,* my internal voice taunted me. *You're a bestselling author of a book all about tidying and organizing. It's only natural that they'd expect you to be a flawless host as well.*

My agents and publishers probably weren't expecting anything beyond a simple business meeting that day. But, seized by panic, I couldn't think straight. You see, even though I always loved keeping a tidy home that sparks joy, I wasn't used to having people over to my home back then. First, I assumed I would need a tea set, which I didn't have with me in my new home. Back when I was single, I didn't own much dishware, and even after I started living with Takumi, my husband, we kept a limited amount, just enough for two. Now, I was suddenly expected to entertain five people.

Okay, tea sets, I told myself. I had no idea what I was doing, but I took myself to a store and came home with eight matching sets of cups and saucers and cake plates. *Wait, what are they going to eat?!*

I ran to a lovely bakery in my neighborhood and quickly purchased a load of pastries and muffins. *What about the table setting?!* I looked at all that I had purchased on my table and thought, *tongs—that's what I need*. I needed a pair of tongs so that I, as the ultimate host, could serve my guests when they arrived.

Looking back, I honestly have no idea what I was thinking. The tongs that I purchased were made of silicone, perfect for vigorously tossing vegetables in a heated wok or boiling some broccoli. Before my guests arrived, I placed the tongs next to the plate of delicate sweets. The image of my guests struggling mightily with the tongs as they tried to serve themselves still makes me cringe. The memory doesn't spark joy.

Thankfully, over the years my hosting skills have improved, and I've grown to enjoy having people over. But I do think that Japanese people—especially when they are abroad—tend to feel uniquely pressured to be the perfect host. We are famous as a nation of people obsessed not only with good food but its meticulous and beautiful presentation (see: chapter 4, Umami). Whenever I invite my American friends or colleagues over, I still can't shake the feeling that somehow they will be disappointed if I don't have a perfect green tea service or homemade sushi platter at the ready. Japan's famous hospitality certainly sets a high bar for every Japanese person.

According to the Japan National Tourism Organization, the number of international visitors to Japan in 2024 reached a record high of 36.9 million, 15.6 percent more visitors than the previous record of 31.9 million in 2019. While there are many reasons to visit the country, no doubt Japan's national commitment to hospitality is at least part of the draw for tourists. When you are a tourist who just landed at Narita or Haneda airport, I wonder what catches your eye first? Perhaps it's the signs that read "*Yokoso!*" or "Welcome!" that seem to decorate every surface of the walls of the arrival gates. I think very few other airports in the world greet you with so many welcome banners. In recent years, both Haneda and Narita airports are also known to have limited-time "welcome campaigns" where the arrival gates are decorated with spectacular displays of internationally beloved anime or video game characters, just in case you feel that your arrival isn't celebrated enough.

While living abroad, whenever I returned to Japan for a visit and stayed at a hotel, one of the little things that instantly made me feel at home was when the concierge, during check-in, pulled out a printed map of the hotel lobby and carefully explains how to find the elevators that would take me up to my room. It's such a small gesture, but it carries a sense of consideration and attentiveness that I associate with the warmth of Japanese hospitality.

Similarly, when I'm out shopping on a rainy day in Tokyo, I experience that familiar sense of care when the shop attendant places a plastic cover over my shopping bag to protect it from the rain. Without fail, they'll accompany me to the store entrance and bow as they see me off, making sure I'm fully taken care of as I leave.

I'm sure many people have had similar moments in Japan. It's the kind of attention to detail that pops up not only at hotels and department stores but also in taxis, grocery stores, restaurants, and even at places like McDonald's. Social media is full of stories of people poking fun at the customer service of Japan, which can sometimes feel over the top when compared to other countries. Most of us aren't regularly treated like royalty in our everyday lives, but the Japanese customer service and instinct for hospitality seem intent on making you feel as close to it as possible, at least for as long as you are a customer. If you ever want to know how it feels to arrive at a place as an important figure, might I suggest a visit to a large department store in Tokyo just as it opens for the day? As you step inside, you're greeted by a chorus of cheerful, synchronized *"Irasshaimase!"* accompanied by deep, respectful bows. It's a level of enthusiasm and precision that can leave tourists in awe, almost as surprising as how meticulously stores in Japan adhere to their opening hours—never a second too early or too late.

In 2013, during the lead-up to the 2020 Summer Olympic and Paralympic Games, the Tokyo Olympic bid ambassador made a speech before the International Olympic Committee using the word *omotenashi*. It went on to become a buzzword both domestically and abroad and no doubt played a part in Tokyo securing the role of host city. The concept of *omotenashi* is key to unpacking the high value Japanese culture places on a warm and thoughtful welcome that we provide for one another.

While there are many theories about the etymology of *omotenashi*, the word is generally understood to be composed of the polite prefix "o" and *motenashi*, which comes from the verb *motenasu* (持て成す), meaning "to accomplish by possessing something." The "something" here points to things both physical and nonphysical, like your heart. Another origin of *omotenashi* is *omoteura nashi* (表裏なし), meaning to be sincere and transparent: literally "without a front and back." Today, *omotenashi* embodies the Japanese idea of doing all that you can to make someone feel welcome with a respectful and earnest heart that does not seek compensation.

The word *motenashi* appears in the Japanese language as far back as the Heian era, and the philosophy and soul behind the word is said to have originated from the tea ceremony that also flourished during this period. A guest to a tea ceremony is expected to consider not only the taste of tea but every detail that surrounds them. This is because everything—from the seasonal flower that adorns the *tokonoma* alcove to the bowl in which the tea is served—has been carefully selected with the

> "In Japan, perfect omotenashi is about being one step ahead of your guests and providing personalized service that even they didn't know they wanted."

guest in mind. As a guest, you are placing yourself in an environment that has been thoughtfully considered so that you can glean the most pleasure from the tea, the room in which you sit, the nature just outside, the season, the day, and the moment. The renowned tea master Sen no Rikyu's approach to tea ceremony embodied the idea of *Ichigo ichie*, which translates to "one time, one meeting."

He believed that every tea ceremony is a singular event, never to be replicated in the same way again. The tea ceremony, by bringing our attention fully to the present, allows us to properly treasure the person with whom we share this fleeting moment in our transient life.

Omotenashi can also be observed in Japan's Shinto rituals. The grounds of a Shinto shrine are carefully cared for, and a breeze seems to always flow through the inside of a shrine. This isn't only for the benefit of human visitors. Shrines are maintained well as a welcoming gesture for the myriad *kami* or deities that reside in Japan. In the past, Japanese people would change furniture and futons into something lighter once summer arrived. This wasn't only so that they could remain cool during the warmer weather. They were making their homes a comfortable place to draw in the seasonal deities. This is why keeping our homes tidy or opening the windows to let the breeze in are still considered a way to attract good fortune and energy into our homes. The many festivities that take place throughout the year in Japan are also a form of *omotenashi* that welcome and entertain the deities in every season.

In English, *omotenashi* is often understood to be synonymous with customer service or hospitality. Yet *omotenashi* is different from a service, which usually incurs a fee, and it is so much more than hospitality, which usually takes place at a specific time and place and for a specific person. *Omotenashi,* on the other hand, concerns your heart and how you choose to express your consideration for another person.

Just the other day, I was dining at a sushi restaurant when it occurred to me that I barely had to ask for anything from the waitress during the entire dinner. After I sat down at my table, the menu was swiftly presented to me exactly when I had lifted my head to ask for it. Before I could realize that my tea had turned a little cold, it was swapped with a fresh brew. As I returned to my seat from the bathroom, a hot *oshibori* hand towel was placed on my table. From beginning to end, not only the food but the consideration the staff had for my needs was impeccable. I couldn't help but ask the waitress how they manage to provide such a thoughtful service.

The waitress dropped her voice to a whisper and said, "At this restaurant, the staff are all trained to observe the customers closely and anticipate their needs before they call for you."

The staff are even encouraged to memorize details

about customers who are regulars, such as their dominant hands, so that they can place glasses and chopsticks on the correct side. They must always ask themselves, "What can I do more to satisfy and bring joy to the customer?" I think in most other countries, it is considered good service when your requests as a customer are met with efficiency and enthusiasm. In Japan, perfect *omotenashi* is about being one step ahead of your guests and providing personalized service that even they didn't know they wanted.

After I finished my dinner at the restaurant, my waitress was already waiting for me at the entrance with my coat, which I had checked when I came in.

"Do you always memorize which coat belongs to which customer?" I asked her.

My waitress smiled and nodded, looking a little embarrassed. The art of *omotenashi* also values subtlety—a thoughtful gesture is best carried out without drawing attention.

Our appreciation for others and a desire to take care of them are not visible to the naked eye. *Omotenashi* encompasses all the efforts that we make to put those invisible feelings into visible actions. There is genuine heart in *omotenashi*.

It's important to remember that *omotenashi* is a two-way street. The goal of *omotenashi* is not for one person to serve another, but to create a sense of harmony from which all parties can benefit and feel good about. *Omotenashi* allows us to connect more deeply with one another.

While I treasure *omotenashi* in Japan, I've also observed a similar spirit in places and cultures other than Japan. Hotel clerks in Europe have inspired me with their witty conversations and bookstore staff in Asia touched my heart with their warm reception. I love the friendliness of people working in restaurants and hotels in the U.S., the confidence with which they share who they are and what they think. While living in the U.S., I've also had the chance to encounter many excellent hosts at public events and home parties. A great host can approach anyone and make them feel at ease. They facilitate conversations and connect people together in a meaningful way. Perhaps my favorite aspect of American hospitality is the joy. Sometimes, in the pursuit of being the perfect host, we can forget that the host should also be having fun.

I like to believe that the word *omotenashi* has captivated the world because, while the word is difficult to define, we intuitively understand what it stands for. *Omotenashi* may look different in each culture, but how wonderful that every culture has a unique way to show someone that they care. We all put a little bit of ourselves—our thoughts, our passions, our wisdom and experiences—into acts of service in hope that they resonate in the heart of another person. *Omotenashi* is something we do for other people, but I always find that it ultimately benefits us. There's no need for a grand gesture to show that you care. It's often the smallest offerings—a tiny vase with a flower on the guest's bedside table, a cold drink on a sweltering day, a big, welcoming hug and a smile as soon as the door opens—that are the most impactful. *Omotenashi* is probably my favorite way to increase my heart's capacity for joy.

CHAPTER 4

Savor
味わう

Umami 旨み

"What does *umami* taste like?"

Back when I started living in the U.S., a friend asked me this question and I couldn't answer it very well. *Umami* isn't exactly sweet or salty . . . My tongue knew the flavor well, but to describe it in words was difficult.

I feel like I've been tasting this flavor nearly every day since I was a child. For example, on nights when I had a cold, my mother would make miso soup. Even if it didn't have many ingredients, the aroma of the *dashi* stock would softly permeate the air, and I felt my body unwinding with every sip. I can never forget that sense of satisfaction that slowly spread within me. Since then, "savoring food" has become more than just satisfying hunger—it's become a way to bring my heart into order. As I grew older and lived abroad, I came to realize that this feeling is, in fact, something deeply Japanese.

In Japan, eating has become a form of entertainment that's deeply woven into daily life.

If you turn on the TV in Japan, there's a good chance you'll catch someone eating. Whether it's slurping a long strand of ramen or udon from a steaming bowl, cutting into a light and fluffy matcha cake, or savoring a piece of tuna so fresh it shines like a gemstone, the scene is always captivating. The camera often lingers on their reactions after the first bite: their eyes close in sheer bliss, followed by a contented groan and the word *"Oishi!,"* which means "Delicious!"

In Japan, the enjoyment of food is a national pastime. A glance at the country's entertainment will reveal an entire genre devoted to pursuing and savoring delicious food. *Oishinbo* is a classic manga series that helped popularize food-related, or "gourmet," manga in Japan. One of the bestselling manga series of all time, *Oishinbo* (a blend of "oishi" and "kuishinbo," a term for someone who loves to eat) ran for over thirty years, from 1983 to 2014. The premise is simple: a cynical food journalist eats his way through a variety of culinary traditions and food cultures in Japan to create the ultimate food guide.

It's hard to imagine a manga centered on its protagonist and his associates simply eating food and deciding whether it's good or not could be thrilling or dramatic, but somehow *Oishinbo* pulls it off. Aimed at adult audiences, the series elevates food to something intellectual, serious, and meaningful. *Oishinbo* is lauded for its deep dive into food production, cooking techniques, and the cultural significance behind various dishes. The fact that Japanese readers devoured over a hundred volumes of this manga— featuring episodes on topics like "The Miracle of Soy Sauce" and "The Secret to *Dashi*"—is a clear testament to the country's profound passion for food.

Japan also has no shortage of TV shows centered around food. From typical cooking programs to game shows, it seems like someone is always talking about food or the latest restaurants opening somewhere in Japan every hour of the day. I once heard that in the West, it's considered somewhat rude or taboo to linger on the image of someone eating for too long. Japanese TV has no such qualms. One of the most nationally popular programs, *Gochi ni Narimasu*, features a group of comedians visiting various high-end restaurants in Tokyo. They order multiple dishes without checking the prices, and whoever comes closest to the show's predetermined total cost wins. For viewers, the fun lies in guessing the price of each dish based on the comedians' reactions to the food they try.

I was in junior high school when I first started watching this show. I remember how excited my family would get as we watched the show together after dinner, guessing the price of each dish. Imagining how good the food must taste and getting excited over the dishes on-screen—such a pastime, I think, is just a natural part of everyday life in Japanese households.

Food-related media in Japan know how to—excuse the pun—*make a meal* out of every slurp, every smack of the lips, and every bead of sweat that forms on our foreheads when we eat something hot. They present food with the utmost care, showcasing its mouthwatering textures, vibrant colors, and every tempting angle. The shows often feature people who have mastered the art of eating, ensuring that viewers can almost taste the food themselves through the screen.

Another beloved, long-running food show is *Kodoku no Gourmet* (Solitary Gourmet), a hit manga series turned

TV drama that's been airing for over a decade. The story follows salaryman Goro Inogashira as he roams Japan, stopping at restaurants and street food stalls to savor local specialties. The series is as stripped down as it gets—each episode focuses on Goro's culinary experiences with little plot to distract from the food. And what a joyous eater Goro is! As he indulges, we hear his unexpectedly poetic and insightful internal monologue about the dishes he's enjoying. It's the ultimate comfort TV, and the series has earned a dedicated fan base in Japan.

The impact of these "gourmet" programs is clear: they inspire people in Japan to seek out the foods or restaurants featured on-screen. Japanese restaurants, cafés, and bars often display signs proudly announcing they've been mentioned in a TV show or manga. It's evident that Japanese people have a genuine love for watching others enjoy food. We deeply empathize with the joy of eating something delicious, and that connection drives us to search for, create, and savor great food ourselves, perpetuating an endless cycle of gastronomic exploration.

Looking back on my upbringing in Japan, I can see how central cooking and food were to my daily life. Though takeout food and delivery services are more common in

Japan today, when I was growing up, there was a general expectation that we would cook and eat three meals a day at home. My mother, a full-time housewife, cooked for our family every day. I feel grateful for the astonishing variety of flavors she introduced me to from an early age and all the effort she must have put into her cooking.

I didn't fully realize how much Japan's food culture had influenced me until I started living abroad. When my children started preschool in the U.S., I had to pack their lunches every day because their school didn't have a cafeteria. Tapping into the memory of what my own mother used to make for me throughout my junior and high school years, I began preparing bento lunches for my daughters. Then, something surprising happened: my daughters reported that their teachers took photos of their bento lunches, gleefully commenting on how cute they looked. I even received compliments when I went to pick them up from school.

Japanese rolled omelette. Sausage shaped like an octopus. Tiny *onigiri* rice balls. Mini tomatoes. Boiled broccoli. The contents of my bento boxes always seemed to delight my daughters' teachers, but their enthusiasm left me feeling deeply embarrassed. I knew my bento didn't live up to the high standards of my home country. Compared to what my mother used to make for me, mine felt simpler and a bit rough around the edges. When I was ten years old, my mother began teaching me how to make a traditional Japanese rolled omelette—because, in Japan, you can't make a bento without knowing how to make one. I remember practicing every day, perfecting the art of rolling thin layers of beaten eggs into a perfect cylindrical shape. My mother taught me that a bento should not only be nutritious but also aesthetically balanced.

The art of bento-making reached new heights with the *kyaraben* craze. This term, which combines the words *kyara* (character) and bento, refers to more than just the cute decorative elements of the bento. It involves the precise re-creation of popular anime characters using rice balls, or the artful arrangement of small animals made from ham and cheese—a world of "edible dioramas," if you will.

Unsatisfied by rows of panda-shaped rice balls, parents started to depict the eyeballs of a Minion with slices of cheese and *nori* seaweed and deployed ketchup to bring the adorable cheeks of a Pikachu to life. Driven only by the hope that their kids would cry out with joy when they opened their bento lunches, parents would go to artistic extremes, moving the edible contents in millimeter units with a tweezer.

Japanese supermarkets and kitchenware stores are packed with tools for turning ordinary bento into *kyaraben*. *Nori* seaweed cutters, molds, silicone cups, and special picks . . . The creative challenge of testing the expressive limits of ingredients, and above all, the desire to see your child happy, fueled this craze.

You're probably thinking, no parent has time for this! And you'd be right. In reality, parents began to voice their despair, saying "It's hell when you oversleep and have no time to prepare," or "I cried over the broken ears of a Pikachu this morning." Soon, the craze began to fizzle out. Some schools sent out letters advising parents not to make *kyaraben* as it invited unnecessary comparisons among children's lunches. A craze that started as a fun pursuit

> "One of the first rules of good manners we learn as children is that before we eat, we should put our hands together, bow our heads slightly, and say, 'Itadakimasu,' which literally translates to 'I will gratefully receive the food.'"

somehow turned into a source of pressure. Sometimes, Japan's passion for food can go a little overboard!

But where does this intense passion for food and cooking come from? I can't help but feel the answer lies in the way Japanese children are raised. I've noticed that when my daughters come home from elementary school, the first thing they talk about—before mentioning their friends or what they did that day—is usually what they ate for lunch. I suspect this is because, in most Japanese elementary schools, lunch is served five days a week, and the menu rarely repeats in the same month. Japanese school lunches typically consist of rice, a soup, a vegetable side, and a protein main dish. While there are set patterns—like curry once a month—variety is the name of the game, which makes each lunch feel like a mini surprise.

In Japan, elementary schools often have nutritionists who calculate the calories and nutrients on a monthly basis, ensuring the meals are well-balanced and support the children's growth. Since one of my daughters has a few food allergies, I'm always impressed by how meticulously her school accommodates her. They remove allergens every time and offer menus that are just as satisfying as what everyone else is enjoying. The school is dedicated to making sure every student, including the teachers, can experience the same meal together.

Japanese elementary schools' approach to food can be summed up in the concept of *shokuiku*, or food education. For example, I've noticed that once or twice a month, my daughters' school serves dishes from around the world, like Spanish omelettes or Korean bibimbap, along with local specialties from different regions of Japan. Students eat these meals while learning about the cultures and traditions behind them. Another common practice in *shokuiku* is letting students grow their own vegetables. Elementary school kids often grow carrots and cabbages at school and then use them in their lunches. Through these hands-on experiences, *shokuiku* nurtures a genuine curiosity about where our food comes from and helps instill a deeper connection to what we eat.

But my favorite—and definitely the most adorable—aspect of Japanese school lunches is how the children serve one another. There are no lunch ladies at Japanese elementary schools. Instead, the students take on the role of servers on a rotating basis. Donning tiny aprons and hats, the servers carry heavy pots of food from the kitchen to the classroom, where they ladle the food onto each tray. Small children don't usually have much control over what they eat at home—they're generally told to eat what's put in front of them, no questions asked. Allowing them to take the proactive role of servers is such a brilliant idea. It's a wonderful way for kids to naturally learn about portion control and how to plate a well-balanced meal. I can still remember my own experience as a server in school, my mind racing as I tried to ladle out the right amount of curry so that everyone got a fair portion.

School lunches in Japan are about so much more than just satisfying hunger—they're an integral part of primary education. From an early age, Japanese children are taught to develop a genuine interest in and appreciation for food—perhaps even a reverence for it. One of the first rules of good manners we learn as children is that before we eat, we should put our hands together, bow our heads slightly, and say, "*Itadakimasu*," which literally translates to "I will gratefully receive the food." This expression of gratitude is not just for the food itself, but for all the lives that contributed to it—the person who cooked it, the farmers and fishermen who provided the ingredients, and the plants, animals, and fruits that made the meal possible. Once the meal is finished, we repeat the same gestures and say, "*Gochisosama deshita*," which is another expression of thanks for all the effort that went into preparing the meal. This ritual of gratitude highlights how food is not just a means of sustenance, but an experience to be respected and celebrated.

This deep attentiveness to food, cultivated from childhood, is reflected in the very essence of Japanese cuisine. One of its hallmarks is the subtle range of flavors that harmonize to create balanced and refined dishes. You've probably heard the term *umami* when discussing Japanese food. While it's gained some fame internationally (*Umami* Burger, anyone?), this distinct flavor was only formally recognized about a century ago in Japan.

Before *umami* was identified, it was believed that humans could only taste four basic sensations: sweet, sour, salty, and bitter. These primary tastes were considered distinct, and you couldn't create one by combining the others. Then, in 1908, Professor Kikunae Ikeda from Tokyo Imperial University (now Tokyo University) uncovered a flavor that didn't fit into any of these categories. He isolated glutamate, an amino acid abundant in kombu seaweed, and named it *umami*, recognizing it as the fifth basic taste. Other Japanese researchers followed suit, discovering additional *umami* components like inosinate in dried bonito flakes and guanylate in shiitake mushrooms.

In recent years, studies on *umami* have expanded globally, revealing that our taste buds have receptors for sweet, sour, salty, bitter, and *umami* sensations. Interestingly, while sweet and salty tastes are primarily detected on the tip of the tongue, *umami* is sensed all over, which could explain why it leaves such a lingering, satisfying impression. In the culinary world, *umami* is celebrated as a powerful flavor enhancer—it's one of the reasons Japanese cuisine can incorporate so many diverse ingredients while keeping calories low. Instead of relying on heavy animal fats, Japanese chefs turn to *umami*-rich broths and stocks, known as *dashi*, to draw out the essence of ingredients. As its health benefits and flavor-enhancing qualities are increasingly recognized, *umami* has become a global culinary trend embraced by chefs worldwide.

Speaking of *umami,* I recently dined at a new restaurant in Kita-Shinagawa, Tokyo, called HONSEN. It's run by three chefs with distinct culinary backgrounds, each blending their expertise to create something truly unique: a fusion of Japanese and French cuisine. The restaurant's seasonal menu pairs expertly with wines, and one dish in particular made my taste buds sit up and take notice. Normally, a carpaccio is served with a side salad or a tangy dressing. But this red clam carpaccio was served together with blanched *nanohana* (rapeseed flowers) soaked in rich, flavorful broth. I hesitated at first—what an unusual pairing!—but then, I tasted it. The moment I took a bite, the *dashi* hit me like a wave. It was light and refreshing, yet impossibly rich with *umami*. It was a flavor I couldn't quite place, but I knew it was something special.

Every dish at HONSEN was bursting with *umami,* and I couldn't help but wonder if the restaurant's head chef, trained in Japanese cuisine, had something to do with it. So, I asked him: *What exactly is umami?*

His answer was unexpected. According to him, the "correct" *umami* can change from day to day. *Umami*, he explained, is fluid, always evolving. What tastes good one day might feel off the next, depending on the temperature or even the humidity. That's why chefs need to communicate with their ingredients—and their customers—to adjust the flavors and bring out the best in every dish.

Talking to him made me think about how sushi chefs

adjust the temperature of their restaurant to match the outside weather, or how they subtly tweak their rice preparation to ensure that it pairs perfectly with the fish. Making food that's truly worth savoring requires being fully present in the moment.

Umami is a flavor that's hard to express with words. But once you experience it, you'll never forget it. It's a subtle flavor, so delicate that it can easily vanish in a dish, but you know when it's there. In Japanese cuisine, *umami* holds the entire meal together, giving it depth and satisfaction.

I can't help but see a metaphor for a way of life in *umami*. *Umami* isn't flashy, but it's something that gently brings comfort to everyday life. It's not about overdoing things, but about engaging with care. I feel that this connects to the essence of what I want to share about bringing a sense of balance into your life.

I hope that my KonMari Method, like *umami*, can be something that quietly nourishes the heart without standing out too much. I have faith that it can help build a foundation for a life meant to be savored.

Utsuwa 器

My enchantment with *utsuwa*—the Japanese word for vessels—began while I was giving my usual lesson in tidying. When we tidy the kitchen, we start by taking all the dishware off the shelves and lining them up, following the KonMari Method. It's quite labor-intensive, a delicate task that requires a great deal of care.

My client took each plate gently in her hands so as not to break it, saying, "This sparks joy" or "You've served your role well. Thank you so much." She was savoring the joy each vessel brought, as if she were conversing with it.

The room was silent, save for the faint sound that echoed each time a new plate prompted whispered words from my client. In the hushed atmosphere, I found myself unable to take my eyes off her collection of dishes. It was as if each plate were a living thing.

I want to clarify that during all of my tidying sessions, I work with the mindset that every object has a will. I can feel that every vessel has its own distinct character and energy, no matter whom it belongs to. I might sense, "This plate has a lot of energy" or "This one is a little tired."

But the dishes that belonged to this particular client seemed imbued with a brilliance that stood out above the rest. They didn't have any flashy designs; if anything, they were mostly white or black—each one a simple, plain dish.

I couldn't help but ask her, "Why do your dishes all look so shiny?"

My client smiled contentedly and said, "Each one is a one-of-a-kind piece made by an artist."

She turned out to be the owner of a gallery that handles tableware and vases by esteemed Japanese ceramic artists.

Why was I so drawn to such a simple white plate? In that moment, I realized the vessel was infused with its maker's aesthetic, passion, and care.

What's more, during a break in our tidying session, my client treated me to a light lunch: some rice, chicken she said she had purchased at a local delicatessen, seasoned grated carrots, and cabbage *ohitashi*. Though seemingly ordinary, once she arranged the food on the simple dishware, each item looked distinct, creating the dignified air of a high-end Japanese restaurant. The power of vessels—the energy poured into an artist's handicrafts—struck me deeply.

Today, most of the dishes I enjoy using every day are made by Japanese artists. I also love the thin, smooth texture of porcelain from a heritage European brand or dishware decorated with delicate artwork. But I believe Japanese pottery has a different quality. While they are vessels that retain the humble texture of earth, they are also remarkably lightweight and durable. Not only that, they feature intricate designs that can only be achieved by hand. I believe that finding an *utsuwa* that merges everyday utility with artisanal beauty is one of the experiences unique to Japan. Behind the creation of such vessels breathes a distinctive Japanese aesthetic sense known as *you no bi* or "the beauty of utility." It's a sensibility that finds beauty not only in surface ornamentation, but in "the act of using something in daily life"—a philosophy that beauty is not confined to galleries and museums, but rather dwells within the ordinary scenes of living.

This way of thinking was first articulated by the Japanese philosopher Soetsu Yanagi in the early 20th century and spread through the Japanese folk crafts or mingei movement. Yanagi taught that within utilitarian objects crafted by unknown artisans, there exists an "anonymous beauty" in which practicality and beauty naturally harmonize. He believed that the true value lies in the nature of vessels: they are quietly cultivated within daily life, their character deepening with use.

The spirit of "the beauty of utility" still thrives today in places where vessels are produced. There are pottery and ceramic kiln sites with different soils, glazes, and techniques across Japan, each with its own tradition and philosophy. Mashiko, Shigaraki, Mino, Karatsu, Bizen, and Arita . . . The character of each kiln, shaped over the years in its unique natural surroundings, is reflected in the vessels, and local craftsmen and artisans complete each piece by hand, pouring their hearts and souls into the process.

The first *utsuwa* made by an artist that I acquired was a white ceramic bowl with a flower-shaped rim, featuring the decorative technique known as *kohiki*, where a layer of white clay is applied to the entire surface of the base clay before another layer of transparent glaze is applied on top.

The mild white color, the texture that rests comfortably in your hands, the petal-shaped rim reminiscent of a flower in bloom—it was love at first sight. The vessel, which seems to change expression as it ages, has taught me the joy of incorporating a piece into my life, which gives it a character beyond beauty.

Another piece I've been using for a long time is a plate made by an artist from Okinawa. The plate, based on ancient pottery from the Ryukyu Kingdom era, features an indigo vine pattern that dances gracefully upon a light greige background, conveying the vitality and suppleness of nature. Just placing a crispy fried egg on top instantly elevates an ordinary breakfast into something special.

I also recently discovered Japanese tableware being used at a restaurant in Los Angeles. The brand, Hasami Porcelain, is a collaboration between a historic porcelain maker from the town of Hasami in Nagasaki Prefecture and designer Takuhiro Shinomoto. Surprisingly, the brand began in the U.S. Inspired by traditional Japanese everyday items such as lacquerware and tiered food boxes (or *jubako*), its matte texture and simple forms—composed solely of straight and curved lines without adornments—highlight functional beauty. Seeing Japanese ceramics that have crossed the ocean and adapted so well to a new environment made me realize that vessels are not simple tools—they bear the imprint of the culture and soul of the place and time in which they were made.

I once had an opportunity to speak with a pottery artist about his work. Our meeting came about in the most unexpected way, and it was unforgettable from the start. When I think of a Japanese ceramic artist, I envision someone dressed in an apron, their hands weathered and worn from years of practice, an old master who has followed the same rigorous path of craftsmanship for decades. This was the image I had in mind when I signed up for a *kintsugi* workshop at a pottery studio one evening.

I followed the address I was given and, to my surprise, found myself in the heart of Omotesando, one of Tokyo's most fashionable districts. After wandering around for a few minutes, unsure of which direction to go, I finally located the building. I walked down a flight of stairs and entered the semi-basement studio. When I opened the door, I was greeted by a tall, slim man—easily over six feet—dressed with such style that I briefly wondered if he was a fashion model or perhaps a designer of some sort.

Taku Nakano reached out to shake my hand and introduced himself as a pottery artist. I looked back at him, speechless. He was dressed entirely in black, with a jagged line of gold running across the front of his sleeveless knitted top, resembling a crack in a piece of pottery. His long, bare arms were covered by black arm covers that extended to his elbows. I glanced down at his feet and noticed he wore a black shoe on his left foot and a solid gold shoe on his right. A pair of gold headphones rested around his neck. He smiled warmly at me from behind his dark, circular sunglasses, which he kept on despite being indoors. He seemed ageless. No, not a fashion model or a designer, I thought to myself. He resembled a character from a science fiction film or perhaps a Tokyo citizen from a hundred years in the future.

Mr. Nakano motioned for me to follow him into the studio. As I entered, I immediately recognized that his space, which he described as a blend of an atelier and a museum, was as unconventional as he was. Sure, there were elements you'd expect in a pottery studio—pottery wheels, worktables covered in clay—but this place felt more like a wizard's workshop or a witch's lair. Vases, goblets, and fluted wineglasses with iridescent glazes shimmered from the tall shelves. A lone tree grew upward into the skylight by the entrance. A tank full of gliding goldfish emitted a blue, ethereal light.

"Growing up, I couldn't find anything I was good at," Mr. Nakano told me after we finished our workshop. "I had no motivation. I had no direction in life."

Mr. Nakano is entirely self-taught, which is unusual in the world of Japanese pottery. Unlike many potters and ceramicists in Japan, who typically apprentice under a master or belong to a specific kiln that follows a long-established style and tradition, Mr. Nakano has carved his own path. He grew up in Awaji-shima, an island in the Seto Inland Sea of Japan. For years, he worked as a typical salaryman, but his life changed when he was transferred to Shizuoka Prefecture. Thanks to its proximity to natural resources like clay and high-quality water, Shizuoka is known for its rich pottery tradition and thriving tea culture. While living there, Mr. Nakano joined a local pottery club on a whim and soon found himself enchanted by the creative possibilities. He was thirty-six years old at the time. Since then, he has been working as a potter and ceramic artist for thirty years.

What stands out about Mr. Nakano's style is that he

developed his own approach to ceramics, allowing him to experiment beyond the confines of traditional techniques. Over time, he discovered that his greatest inspiration came from something familiar to him throughout his life: the starlit night sky of his hometown in Awaji-shima. Captivated by the beauty of the galaxy, the glimmer of a shooting star, and the mystery of the moon, he sought to express these wonders through his work. Now I understood why so many of Mr. Nakano's original pieces were unlike any pottery I had seen before. The extraterrestrial influences in his work were immediately apparent. His tableware, both visually and metaphorically, resembled distant planets. Mr. Nakano reminded me that the elements he uses in his work—metals like gold, platinum, and silver—are thought to have been formed in extreme cosmic events.

> "While utsuwa (器) literally refers to a vessel or container, it can also be used metaphorically to describe a person's internal capacity to handle different aspects of life or situations."

"Some people create a piece of pottery to serve a specific purpose," he explained, "but when I create something, I'm searching for new possibilities and challenges. The vessels that emerge change me, not the other way around. If I'm trying to make a piece with the galaxy or constellations as its motif, for example, it drives me to study and learn about them. It's like I'm competing with the piece or engaging in a dialogue with it. I want to be worthy of the vessel I'm making. It challenges me to push my own potential further."

Listening to him, I was reminded of the nuanced meaning of the Japanese word for vessel. While *utsuwa* (器) literally refers to a vessel or container, it can also be used metaphorically to describe a person's internal capacity to handle different aspects of life or situations. For example, a person with a "large *utsuwa*" (okina *utsuwa*) would be capable, open-minded, or able to handle difficult situations with grace.

Mr. Nakano then asked if I had ever thought about the deeper meaning of *utsuwa*. "'Utsu' means emptiness or a void, 'wa' symbolizes a circular shape, like a ring or a wheel," he explained. "It's only because *utsuwa* is empty that it can be filled with something. It's not complete unless there's something inside, and its form and appearance can change depending on what's inside."

I realized then that many Japanese words that refer to change also have *utsu* as their root. For instance, there's *utsuroi* (移ろい), which means change, transition, or impermanence. It often refers to the natural, gradual process of things changing or fading over time, such as the changing of seasons, the passage of time, or the shifting of emotions. Sure, there's sadness associated with change and impermanence, but *utsu* also points to the limitless potential of empty space.

In Japanese Shinto tradition, empty space can be transformed into a temporary sanctuary for a divine spirit. This sanctuary, known as a *himorogi*, is typically a square area marked by placing poles—such as green branches or bamboo—at the four corners. A rope, called *shimenawa*, is then strung between the poles, designating the empty space inside as a sacred site. In Japanese culture, a void is rarely an absence. The rituals we perform imbue that emptiness with meaning and purpose. In the past, Japanese people also considered their homes sacred spaces. While we no longer give much thought to removing our shoes before entering a home, this simple act of purification was once a vital ritual, marking the transition into a space considered sacred.

As a professional tidying consultant, I've had the privilege of visiting homes across a variety of settings. I often think fondly of the spaces I've visited and tidied. A small apartment in the suburbs of Tokyo. A mansion with a pool in Los Angeles. An editorial office overlooking the skyline of Manhattan. Over the last decade, after the publication of my first book, I've moved often, calling many different hotels and houses my home. But no matter where I find myself, I always make sure to designate specific spots for my belongings. I like to put out fresh flowers whenever I can. When I need a burst of energy, I spritz a few sprays of my favorite scent into the air. Whether in a hotel room in London or a temporary home in California, I always try to make every space I inhabit meaningful.

When you think about it, our houses are like vessels, with nothing but empty space inside. What turns a house into a home? It's the time we spend there, the emotions, events, and memories we attach to it, that give meaning to the space. This, I believe, is why I find tidying a home so important. Tidying is a way to care for the vessel that holds our precious daily lives, allowing us to fully appreciate the moments we spend within it.

As we've seen, the essential function of vessels is to

contain something. That something can be as big as our lives or as small as a single meal. But in both cases, it's important to think about how the vessel itself harmonizes with what's inside it. For example, a black rice bowl brings out the beauty of white rice. A black mug, on the other hand, doesn't quite work for green tea. I feel that the transparent green of the tea calls for none other than a light-colored traditional Japanese teacup. Considering how a vessel interacts with what's inside it can enhance both the function and beauty of the vessel.

This idea can be readily observed in Japanese cuisine, which has an intimate relationship with vessels. The core values of traditional Japanese cuisine—such as aesthetics, tradition, and seasonality—are reflected not only in flavor but also in the vessel and arrangement of each dish. Yuki Teiichi, the founder of the legendary restaurant Kitcho in Osaka, who is credited with popularizing the multicourse kaiseki meal in Japan, once wrote that a vessel can make or break the quality of Japanese cuisine. He compared selecting the right vessel to choosing the backdrop in a *kabuki* theater. A solid black or pale yellow backdrop in *kabuki* is designed to enhance the performance or the actor's costume. The same principle applies to vessels.

A professional Japanese chef spends years training to tell a story through food. Often, that story revolves around seasonality. The four distinct seasons in Japan offer ingredients for chefs to work with, but they also reflect the seasonal transformations through vessels. Traditional celebrations and festivals in Japan are closely tied to the seasons, so chefs might choose special vessels reserved for particular occasions. For example, a traditional stacked bento box, called *jubako*, is used during New Year celebrations. Vessels adorned with cherry blossom patterns are common in spring, while red or yellow vessels reminiscent of the Japanese maple tree appear in autumn. Chefs also know how to harmonize with the season through vessels with the right texture, color, and shape. A cooling dish in the height of summer might be presented in a chilled glass bowl, while a hot meal during winter might be served in clay-fired pottery that feels warm and earthy.

From pottery and porcelain to lacquerware, vessels produced in Japan reflect the resources and traditions of different regions across the country. These vessels are tools for professional chefs, who are said to sometimes select dishware based on the mood or state of mind they perceive from their customers. However, *utsuwa* are also designed with practicality in mind—they are meant for everyday use. For instance, even Japanese children just beginning to eat a variety of foods are often served miso soup in small, lacquered bowls. I can't think of a better way to learn how to savor a meal than by cupping a hot bowl of soup that allows one to feel and appreciate the beauty of the wood from which it's crafted.

Recently, I've heard that pottery and ceramic classes are becoming popular in many global cities, especially among young people. I've also tried pottery with my children, so I can understand the appeal. There is value in making something one-of-a-kind that's meaningful to you, especially at a time when so many things are mass-produced. We may live in a world where everything is at our fingertips, but how many of those things truly carry our souls? How many of them teach us to savor the moment?

One of the most curious things I've noticed while tidying my clients' homes is how we all tend to store our finest tableware away for "special occasions." Dishware that's tucked away for safekeeping is often forgotten or never used—and that's a shame. I believe that something we love can be a powerful catalyst for change. Using a special bowl you cherish can inspire you to cook at home or finally try that recipe you've been meaning to attempt. It might even encourage you to invite friends over for dinner. You might find yourself looking at your meal differently, with a renewed appreciation and love for the things and people around your table. To me, savoring something is about giving personal meaning to our lives.

Reach into the back of that top shelf in your kitchen and take out that *utsuwa* you've been saving for a special night. That special night is tonight! You don't need permission to add a spark of joy to your life, but if you feel you need one, here it is from me. Use the *utsuwa* to serve dinner tonight and see what wonderful things come of it.

Onigiri おにぎり

Onigiri is Japan's soul food. It's a simple dish made by shaping steamed rice with your hands. The name *onigiri* derives from the verb *nigiru* (握る), meaning to grasp or squeeze something. Most *onigiri* are shaped into a triangular form before they are wrapped with crisp dried sheets of *nori* seaweed. The rice balls can be stuffed with a variety of delicious fillings and flavors.

Whenever I traveled abroad for work, I felt as if I was constantly searching for rice balls. During lunch breaks, people would approach me and kindly ask, "What would you like to eat for lunch?" Most of the time, even though I knew it would be next to impossible to find them, I'd answer in my head, "*Onigiri*."

My need for rice balls took on a renewed urgency when I officially began living in the U.S. The first place I moved to from Japan was Palo Alto, California. My publisher was based in San Francisico so I often visited the city and wandered around like a tourist. Even as I enjoyed my new home, I could never last too long without Japanese food, particularly rice balls. In San Francisco, there was a shop called Onigilly, and I don't know how many times their rice balls saved me.

Just like sandwiches, *onigiri* are easy to make, healthy, and portable. They're equally at home in children's lunchboxes and on picnics. What I love about *onigiri* is not just their deliciousness, but also their appearance. The simple yet cute design—a plump white triangle with a little bit of seaweed—soothes my heart just by looking at it. When I dressed my three-year-old son in a T-shirt with an *onigiri* design, it melted the hearts of everyone we encountered, and he himself was in a good mood. Whenever I come across accessories with *onigiri* motifs like *onigiri* pouches or bags, I can't help but murmur "*kawaii.*"

It's my personal belief that the secret to making delicious *onigiri* isn't the choice of filling or how perfectly you shape them—it's the love and energy you send into an *onigiri* with your hands. You have to keep the person who will eat your *onigiri* in mind while lovingly shaping it with your hands.

These days, people understandably prefer to wear gloves when cooking, especially in a professional setting. Even before the pandemic, it was commonplace for chefs in most American restaurants to wear gloves when preparing rice balls. In Japan, the antithesis of the *onigiri*, called *onigirazu*, which literally means "to *not* grasp or squeeze," became a hit in recent years as a new style of *onigiri* that suited our busy contemporary lifestyle. This type of rice ball resembles a burrito or a sandwich, with a sheet of *nori* wrapping the rice and ingredients together.

> "Onigiri is Japan's soul food. It's a simple dish made by shaping steamed rice with your hands."

This eliminates the need to squeeze the rice with your hands. I've never made *onigirazu* myself, but I have used plastic wrap to make *onigiri*. I understand it's a necessary concession that reflects the times we are living in. Nevertheless, I stand firm in my belief that when it comes to *onigiri*, nothing beats making them by hand.

In fact, *onigiri* has an alternative name: *omusubi*. The word comes from the verb *musubu* (結ぶ), meaning "to bind." The word usually expresses the bond or fate that ties people together. *Onigiri*, or *omusubi*, could be said to symbolize the act of binding—the connection between people through nourishment. The idea of binding rice together with love strikes me as a uniquely Japanese culinary concept.

Rice balls are the ultimate comfort food because when they are made with care, you can literally taste the difference. Rice balls bind not only the eater and the maker but also connect us to the ingredients and the sources in nature that made them all possible. This act of binding carries more meaning than just cooking.

My favorite type of rice ball is *shio-musubi* or salted rice balls. For me, there's nothing better than the flavor of the rice's sweetness, the savory taste of salt, and the fragrant *nori* seaweed coming together in perfect harmony. Of course, a delectable salted rice ball cannot be made without quality salt. The brand of salt I love to use is called Zayu no Shio, a sea salt made by the salt artisan Yuzen Inoue. I will introduce his story more in detail later. Mr. Inoue has another type of salt, literally named "Salt that Turns

Rice Balls into a Treat," for which he collaborated with my good friend and rice ball expert, Kana Sugamoto. Their collaboration product blends mineral-rich sea salt from the Yuya Bay in Yamaguchi Prefecture with *akamoku* seaweed, a superfood rich in dietary fiber. The smoked salt has a mouthwatering aroma and depth, and when you make rice balls with it, you feel as if the rice had been slowly cooked outside in a *kamado*, or a traditional Japanese stove.

I'd like to tell you a bit about Kana. As a traveling rice ball vendor, she has visited all forty-seven prefectures of Japan to study the different ways rice balls are prepared in each region. Kana suffered from an eating disorder in her teens, and she credits *onigiri* as what saved her from a difficult time in her life. Today, she celebrates the joy of eating and the food cultures of Japan through rice balls. Her story is a reminder that healthy food is a great source of healing and joy.

Before I met Kana, I used to prefer the classic ingredients for my rice balls: pickled plum, salmon, and kombu. But Kana has opened my eyes to the vast array of regional recipes, which shows that there are really no limits to the ingredients that can be used to fill a rice ball.

Some that piqued my interest include eggplant and miso rice balls, bacon and asparagus rice balls, and kashiwa-meshi rice balls, a Kyushu region specialty made with traditional chicken rice blended with flavorful vegetables, burdock roots, and mushrooms. Kana also recommends oyster *onigiri* from Miyagi Prefecture. In Tokushima Prefecture, there's even a rice ball with sudachi, a green citrus fruit!

I think what brought us together as friends was that we both believe in the healing power of human touch. Not everyone immediately takes to the idea that we can pour our love into something through our hands. Just as I feel that it's possible to send love through my hands when folding clothes, Kana understands that rice balls are comforting and nourishing because of how they are made, cradled in our palms with love.

It's uncanny how the character of rice balls can change depending on the person making them. My children also love rice balls, especially ones made by my husband, Takumi. Takumi's hands are large, so his *onigiri* are extra big, too. My children call them "papa-nigiri," and they are beloved in our house for their robust size and energy.

The rice balls I make are much smaller—perhaps a

third of Takumi's *onigiri*—and are rather delicate and easy on the stomach. My children tell me they are perfect for those times when they are full but still craving a little something more. Rice balls are deceptively simple to make, but they crystallize the essence of food and cooking: warmth, community, and above all, connection.

I hope that this has put you in the mood to try your own hands at making *onigiri*. As a special treat, Kana has shared with us two rice ball recipes, which also happen to be my favorites. Now, you might think that rice balls are as easy and fundamental as Japanese cooking goes. But remember: never underestimate the role that your hands play in making rice balls. If you work through each step in these recipes with enough care and love, you'll be sure to taste the difference.

ULTIMATE SALT ONIGIRI RECIPE
(Makes 3)

Ingredients

- Freshly cooked rice: 300g/10.5oz
  (about 1 cup)
- Natural salt (coarse salt
  recommended): about 1/3 teaspoon
- Hand-toasted *nori* seaweed (optional):
  3 pieces (1/3 size of a full sheet each)

Instructions

1. **Wash the rice**

   Gently pour water into a bowl of uncooked rice,
   then drain immediately (rice absorbs the first water it
   contacts with most, so drain while the water is
   still clean)

   Stir the rice about 20 times in a circular motion with
   your fingers, pour in water and drain quickly. Repeat
   this washing and draining process about 2 more times

   After washing, pour water into the bowl and let the
   rice soak for 30 minutes to 1 hour. (Soaking is not
   necessary if using a rice cooker)

2. **Cook the rice**

   Use slightly less water than usual, add a pinch of salt (not counted in the ingredients list), cook the rice and let it steam for 15 minutes

3. **Prepare before shaping the *onigiri***

   Wet your hands with water, clap them about twice to remove excess moisture

   Take a pinch of salt with three fingertips and sprinkle it over your entire palm

   Take about 100g of warm rice in your hand (if the rice is too hot, first put it in a bowl to cool slightly)

4. **Shape the *onigiri* (this is the key point!)**

   Use your left hand to control the thickness and your right hand to shape the *onigiri* (reverse if left-handed)

   Gently form the rice without crushing the grains. Use slightly less pressure than a handshake. Try not to reshape too many times; aim for about 6 motions

5. **Finishing**

   If using *nori*, wrap it just before eating

   Even without *nori*, the charm of salt *onigiri* stands out

SALMON ONIGIRI

(Makes 3)

Ingredients

- Freshly cooked rice: 300g/10.5oz
  (about 1 cup)
- Natural salt (coarse salt
  recommended): about 1/3 teaspoon
- Salmon: about 100g
- Hand-toasted *nori* seaweed: 3 pieces
  (1/3 size of a full sheet each)

Instructions

1. **Cook the salmon**

   Lightly salt the salmon, wipe off excess moisture,
   cook in a lightly oiled frying pan, then remove bones
   and flake the meat

2. **Wash the rice ~ Prepare before shaping**

   Follow the salt *onigiri* instructions. You can use
   slightly less rice than for plain salt *onigiri* since you'll
   be adding filling

3. **Shape the *onigiri***

   Place 1/3 of the flaked salmon in the middle of the
   rice and shape the *onigiri*. If it's difficult to add filling
   while the rice is in your palm, you can place salmon
   in the middle of rice in a bowl, then transfer to your
   palm to shape

4. **Finishing**

   Wrap with *nori*

   You can also top the *onigiri* with some salmon

Variations

- Try mixing the flaked salmon with warm rice
  before shaping. You can add white sesame seeds,
  cheese, scrambled eggs, salt-massaged cucumber,
  or other ingredients to add flavor, variety,
  and color

CHAPTER 5

Purify
清める

Joka 浄化

What is your ideal morning routine? Here's mine. First, I wake up and open the windows one by one in each room, as if I'm gently waking up my home. Then, it's time to burn incense. My current incense of choice is frankincense, and after I light it, I like to take a quiet moment to watch the wispy column of smoke rise into the air. I love this small moment in my day, when I breathe in the fragrance and stare in wonder at the little incense that manages to cleanse my home every morning without fail.

Then, I take myself to the entrance, an important part of the home where things, people, and maybe even different energies come and go. In Japan, we call the area just inside the entrance where people remove their shoes the *tataki*. I take special care to keep this space spick-and-span. While I'm at it, I also clean and tidy the shoes before putting them back in the shoe rack, then finish by burning some incense to refresh the entrance area.

Cleansing rituals are something I incorporate intentionally into my everyday life. There are moments when I feel particularly run-down or unsettled in my mind and body. Perhaps work isn't going as well as it should. Whenever I feel this way, I take it as a sign that it's time to clear the air. Returning to a clean slate in my mind and spirit is important to me. I believe that what you want to do and what you should do are intuitions that should rise naturally out of us. So when those intuitions—our inner voice—are blocked, it means there are extraneous things getting in the way, preventing us from being entirely ourselves.

Japan is a country that cherishes the rituals of purification. These rituals were all around me as I grew up in Japan, and without even being aware of their significance or meaning, they became a part of my life.

Kodo (香道), or the Way of Incense, is considered one of the classical Japanese arts, along with *Chado* (茶道), the Way of Tea, and *Kado* (華道), the Way of

Flowers. The *Nihon Shoki*, one of the oldest official chronicles of Japanese history, recorded the discovery of aromatic wood over 1,400 years ago when a large piece of agarwood washed ashore on Awaji Island. The beginning of incense use in Japan is closely tied to the introduction of Buddhism. From an integral part of religious rituals, the appreciation of aromatic woods developed into a refined cultural practice. The formal procedures and rules of what we know as *Kodo* today were established during the Muromachi period (1336–1573).

I was also fascinated to learn that military commanders of Japan's Warring States era (1467–1615) would participate in the art of incense and tea amidst warfare. One of my favorite scents is *kuromoji*, a tree from the camphor family native to Japan. Although I only discovered it about ten years ago, it's actually one of Japan's most traditional and time-honored fragrances. The tea master Sen no Rikyu is thought to have used *kuromoji* to calm the turbulent hearts of warriors who came to participate in a tea ceremony with Rikyu, who provided a temporary moment of solace from the bloodshed. Just a hint of the *kuromoji* fragrance can give you a cleansing sensation that resonates deeply in the mind. It's peppery and refreshing at first, with a rich fullness that unfolds later. It's a perfect fragrance for meditation. I use it as a room spray or as an essential oil, relying upon its ability to soothe the soul and clarify whatever is cluttering my mind.

Another purification ritual I love involves sound. If you have seen my Netflix shows, you might have seen me holding a sound tuner and a small piece of crystal. When you gently strike the tuner with the crystal, it chimes brightly. I use the sound tuner at the beginning of a tidying session, or even during, if my client and I are feeling tired and need a quick refresh. The tuner's melodic ring helps us shift our mindset. After I strike the tuner, I like to circle it around my head or up and down my body, as if to let the vibration of the sound resonate into me. It helps me feel more centered and in tune.

When we feel unsettled, our minds are usually overworked. "What should I do about that?" "What's going to happen with this?" The sound of the tuner cuts through such worries and anxieties, stopping all thoughts for a moment. My mind grows still, until, out of the quiet void, comes an answer. I always have faith that our intuition will come to us as long as we clear the way.

Purifying sounds are part of daily life in Japan. When

you walk into a Buddhist temple, you might hear the chanting of the sutra, which is believed to have spiritual power. At a Shinto shrine, you'll hear the crunch of gravel underfoot as you walk the long approach. This type of decorative gravel or pebbles is called *tama-jari* (玉砂利), often found in Shinto shrines, temple grounds, and grave sites. The word *tama* (玉) means jewel, gem, or a soul. Larger than regular gravel, *tama-jari* are round and uniform with no sharp edges. It's said that the sound of stepping on *tama-jari* drives away evil spirits. And it's true: as you walk into a shrine, each step accompanied by that soft, steady sound, you start to feel a sense of calm. Your heart settles and lets you know you've entered a sacred place.

The ceremonial clapping, known as *hakushu* or *kashiwade* (拍手), is a traditional Shinto practice used when paying respects to the *kami* (deities or spirits) at a shrine. I first noticed the purifying effects of ceremonial clapping when I worked as a shrine maiden. When you think about it, clapping with your hands is a simple act that creates such a vibrant, resonant sound. I felt it changed the mood, and even before I knew about sound tuners, I incorporated the practice into my tidying sessions. Whenever I saw my clients struggling or feeling unsure, I would clap my hands, letting the sound give a different energy to the space.

Things that have long been unused need to be woken up before we can begin sorting and tidying them. For instance, when we tidy books, I always ask clients to take out all the books they own off the shelves. You can't choose which books spark joy just by gazing at them. Once my client has taken out their entire literary collection, sometimes I go around patting the surface of the books, almost like a light tap on the cheek, or I'll clap my hands before the towering piles. This is all done to awaken the books.

"Having a purified crystal on my person, placing one in my room, or simply rolling a small piece of crystal around the back of my neck or my back helps soothe that feeling of heaviness."

Of course, more often than not, my clients stare at me in startled confusion as I tap away at their books. No matter. You'd be surprised to know how many people have actually confessed to me that after I performed my little magical ritual, it made it easier for them to choose what sparks joy!

In Buddhism, one of the most iconic rituals involving sound is *Joya no Kane* (除夜の鐘), the traditional ringing of temple bells in Japan on New Year's Eve. When I hear that low, solemn gong reverberate through my neighborhood, it puts me in a reflective mindset, and I know that another year is coming to a close. The long, echoing hum always seems to slow down time, allowing me to appreciate each passing minute. The temple's massive bronze bell is struck 108 times with a wooden beam, symbolizing the earthly desires (*bonno*, 煩悩) that are believed in Buddhism to cloud the mind. Each symbolic strike is meant to cleanse the spirit of such desires so that you can start the new year fresh.

In addition to annual purification rituals, I sometimes crave a more thorough cleanse to refresh myself from head to toe. I reserve these special purification practices for times when I've completed an unusually intense series of work projects, when I haven't been able to keep up with my daily cleansing rituals, or when I return to Japan after being away for a while.

The Fukagawa Fudo-do, a Buddhist temple in the historic Fukagawa neighborhood of Tokyo, is famous for its daily *Goma-daki* (護摩焚き) or Goma fire rituals.

Inside the temple hall, a priest burns wooden sticks in a sacred fire to purify negative energies, thoughts, and desires. The experience, with the visual spectacle of a tall column of fire rising before you combined with the accelerating beat of the taiko drums and the chanting by the priests, is incredibly powerful and exhilarating. It's a moment that stimulates all of your five senses at once.

During the ritual, you can choose to have an item of personal belongings, such as a handbag, purified by a priest, who will offer it near the fire. While Fukagawa Fudō-dō is my go-to when I'm in Tokyo, other temples across Japan offer the ritual as well. I highly recommend the experience. Of course, I don't know if there's any scientific evidence to support its effects, but afterward I do feel much lighter, with a purer sense of myself.

One cleansing ritual that I am able to practice no matter where I am involves crystals. In my home, crystals are essential. I keep a large crystal, about 25 cm wide and 20 cm tall, a beautiful piece that I fell in love with while in the U.S. I also keep a crystal in my study and three rose quartz orbs on my dresser. I have a few portable crystals for when I'm out and about, and a crystal bracelet and necklace that I occasionally wear.

I love crystals simply because they look lovely. It's nice to have something beautiful and sparkling as part of your interior decor. Even if someone told me that bronze statues in a temple have amazing cleansing effects, it would be too impactful to put one inside my home. But a crystal can adapt to a normal living space. And I stand by the fact that the room looks much tidier with a crystal than without it!

I began to sense the positive effects crystals had on me around the time I published my first book. My life had suddenly become inundated with tapings for TV shows and magazine interviews on top of the regular tidying lessons with my clients and my writing. My schedule was completely full, and I was feeling a bit worn out.

Being exposed in the media and meeting many people every day demands a lot from a person's energy. One night, around eight o'clock, I remember feeling suddenly heavy, my whole body and spirit drained of life. I realized then that it was exactly the time a very popular TV program I had appeared in was supposed to air. Somehow, in the back of my mind, I must have been aware of it, and the anxiety and the pressure manifested in me as a heaviness unlike anything I had ever experienced.

In those days, I had an uncanny ability to notice the joy as well as its opposite in people and things, even if it wasn't apparent on the surface. I knew when things or people were in need of a little rest. Perhaps my experience of giving tidying lessons nearly every day had honed my "spark joy sensor" to its limits. But I had overlooked the weakened state of my own energy and soul.

Having a purified crystal on my person, placing one in my room, or simply rolling a small piece of crystal around the back of my neck or my back helps soothe that feeling of heaviness. You could call it a good-luck charm, but for me, crystals really do wonders.

Looking back on my life, I can remember a time when I was the most spiritually cleansed. It was way back in my past, even before I thought about writing books about tidying. I was still living in my parents' home. With time at my leisure, I could begin my day by wiping down the entryway floor. Before I went to sleep, I would also make sure my bedroom was entirely free of dust, which tends to accumulate easily in Tokyo. Keeping tidy was much easier because my personal space in my parents' home was limited to my room. Once or twice a month, I would even do a deep clean, vacuuming inside every inch of my drawers.

I was meticulous about keeping my living environment as clear as possible.

I was still working full-time at a company back then, and I was dedicated to keeping my workplace just as tidy as my home. Every morning when I got to the office (I was often the first to arrive), I'd take my favorite cloth to wipe down my desk, the phone, and my computer. I'd even crawl under the desk and quickly clean the legs of the desk, the cords underneath, and even the legs of my chair. I was studying feng shui at the time and had just learned that keeping your workspace clean led to good fortune and improved productivity, so I was eager to try it. Needless to say, with all this cleansing, I felt thoroughly purified both in mind and spirit. My sensitivity to joy was as sharp as it could be, and I knew exactly what I did and did not want to do and where I was going in life.

The truth is, this supreme level of cleansing has become a gold standard for me, and I'm rather nostalgic for how it felt to be so purified. I could go to the shrine every day if I wanted to, and I felt that luck was always on my side. These days, I live in my own home with my family. As my three children grow up, their belongings multiply and get bigger in size. With a family and a career, I have less time to devote to the cleansing rituals that I was so dedicated to practicing in the past. I know that in the absence of perfection, there is something so much more available for me today. There are joyous moments with my children. While there are more things in my home, these things include books and toys that nurture my children's sense of beauty, wonder, and curiosity. These new realities of my life give me the confidence that where I am is the best possible place to be for me, right now.

Purification rituals that calm my mind and give me a sense of peace remain an indispensable support in my life. Even if there are fewer days when I can do it perfectly—or exactly the way I envision—they always bring me back to my true self. Every time I reclaim a sense of clarity in my daily life, I become just a little bit more centered.

Shio 塩

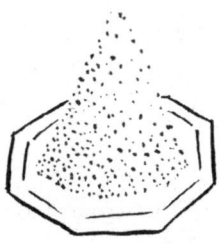

One thing I can tell you about a typical day in my life is that it's very . . . salty.

An essential step in my morning routine is to drink a cup of *sayu* with a pinch of salt. *Sayu*, in Japanese, refers to boiled hot water, typically consumed after it has cooled. I used to drink this cup of hot water without adding anything, but I read that sprinkling a little salt into *sayu* helps the body absorb the water more efficiently, so I decided to try it. It's a subtle difference, but drinking this small concoction rejuvenates me, providing my body with the hydration it needs to start the day.

The next thing I always do is tidy my small household shrine, the *kamidana*. According to Shinto beliefs, there are three basic items you should place on an altar as an offering to the deity or *kami* that watches over your home: water, rice, and salt. Every morning, I replace the water in the vase holding a branch of *sasaki*, a sacred evergreen, and I also refresh the small bowls of rice and salt with new ones. After that, I prepare breakfast for my family, and of course, salt is always a key ingredient.

In the thermos I carry around during the day you'll most likely find *sayu* with a pinch of salt. I used to take hot tea on the go, but since I recently decided to properly enjoy my teatime at home, I switched to hot water with salt to stay hydrated throughout the day. I even keep stick-sized packets of salt in my purse when I go on business trips.

After a long day, I enjoy a bath with bath salts. On days when I feel especially tired or my body feels heavy—like after meeting many people or giving a presentation to a large audience—I do a full salt cleanse. This involves massaging salt all over my body or sometimes just focusing on the backs of my feet. If that's not enough and I need a full refresh, I take a handful of salt, place it on the top of my head, and then shower from head to toe. Does that sound intense? Maybe. But trust me, it works. I slather myself with salt, and by the end, my whole body feels completely purified.

In my bedroom, I keep a pink Himalayan rock salt lamp. The soft, rosy glow soothes me every night, helping me ease into a restful sleep. As you can probably tell by now, salt is far more than just a simple seasoning for me. It helps put my body and mind in order and purifies my energy—it's an essential part of my daily life. You could even say it's my life force. The presence of salt alone makes me feel calmer.

I'm hardly the only Japanese person who praises salt. In Japan, salt plays a symbolic role in purification, protection, and sanctity. It is considered a powerful purifying agent, capable of warding off evil spirits and maintaining both spiritual and physical cleanliness. If you've ever watched a sumo match, you may have noticed the wrestlers tossing fistfuls of salt across the ring. Sumo has been closely tied to Shinto religion throughout its history. Originally, sumo matches were held on the grounds of a Shinto shrine, and the wrestling ring, called *basho* (場所), is still regarded as a sacred space. This is why wrestlers purify the area with salt before a match—hoping for protection and to drive away negative spirits.

In Japan, if you pay close attention to the entrance of

residential homes, restaurants, or shrines, you will start to notice two small mounds of salt, typically placed in small bowls, set out on either side of entryways. Known as *morishio* (盛り塩), this practice is meant to purify the space and protect it from evil spirits. Restaurants and shops may also place them at the entrance to attract prosperity and good fortune. I consider homes—whether my own or others'—to be sacred spaces worthy of our highest respect. That's why I've developed ways to incorporate the use of salt into my own tidying method.

When tidying our homes, certain items are much harder to part with than others. Typically, these are sentimental items or memorabilia. I've often seen clients struggle to let go of items that trigger emotions and memories, even when they truly want to. That's when I take out a special packet of salt I use while tidying. As a symbolic gesture, sprinkling a bit of salt on items being let go helps clients release any lingering emotions or memories attached to those items, allowing them to move forward with a clean slate. Without forgetting to express gratitude for the item—whether it's a letter, a photograph, or something else—I guide clients to place it in an envelope with a sprinkle of salt before letting it go.

Of course, to fully appreciate the gift of salt, you can't forget to enjoy it as a seasoning. Over the years, I've tried many kinds of salt and become quite the connoisseur. Among them, there's one particular salt that captivated me so deeply that I went to meet the person who makes it. To visit the salt artisan, Yuzen Inoue, I traveled to Yamaguchi Prefecture, where I drove along the prefecture's stunning coastline. Soon, I noticed the path I was on began to turn into rugged terrain through a mountain. My car bounced up and down, and I had no idea where the road was leading me—until, all at once, the vision before me opened up to reveal the vast, tranquil sea.

In that moment, I felt that the long journey had led me not only to the ocean but to something far more essential that transcends time.

I had reached Yuya Island, located at the tip of the Mukatsuku Peninsula in Nagato City, Yamaguchi Prefecture. The island sits in Yuya Bay, a calm inlet that faces the Sea of Japan.

Mr. Yuzen Inoue, the salt master, had traveled across Japan tasting seawater before he finally discovered Yuya Bay. Normally, seawater is too bitter to drink, but he found that the water surrounding the bay is mild enough to sip.

Since then, he has devoted twenty years to producing salt from the waters of the bay.

"The most important deciding factor in the flavor of salt is rain," he explained. "The rain falls on the forest and carries the nutrients from the forest into the river, which then flows into the sea. This gives the seawater a distinctive *umami* flavor. The more this cycle occurs, the better it is, as it creates what is known as the brackish water zone, providing the ideal conditions for producing salt."

> "Salt is far more than just a simple seasoning for me. It helps put my body and mind in order and purifies my energy — it's an essential part of my daily life."

Over fifty percent of the area around Yuya Bay, known as a "natural harbor" since ancient times, is covered with a primeval forest. Two rivers, the Awano River and the Kakebuchi River, flow into the bay from within Nagato City. The seawater in the bay combines the nutrients from the mountains with the minerals from the sea, making it possible to create a salt that distills the blessings of both the sea and the mountains.

Looking around the bay, it seemed to me as though the only thing for miles was Mr. Inoue's salt workshop. But he is accustomed to a life far removed from modern conveniences. Mr. Inoue, who grew up in Yamaguchi Prefecture, began working for a major corporation in Tokyo after graduating from his local high school. In Tokyo, he experienced an electrical blackout caused by a typhoon that halted nearly all the functions of the city. It was then that he realized how dependent people had become on modern technology. Driven by an interest in a more sustainable, self-sufficient lifestyle, he returned to his home prefecture. In his twenties, he began living in the mountains and growing his own food to survive. This experience opened his eyes to the vital role salt plays as a daily necessity. Even the food he was growing from scratch wouldn't be worthwhile if the salt he used wasn't safe and of high quality. Motivated by a desire to produce his own salt, he began touring salt fields across Japan.

All salt in Japan is harvested from the sea. The country has no natural resources like rock salt deposits or salt lakes, so Japanese salt production typically involves boiling seawater to extract salt crystals. Since the concentration of dissolved salt in seawater is only about three percent, simply boiling seawater is a labor-intensive process. Japan's humid climate also causes the water to take much longer to evaporate. Throughout history, the Japanese people have had to use a great deal of wisdom and ingenuity to develop efficient ways to produce concentrated saltwater.

Given this background, stabilizing salt production and its price has been a significant concern for the Japanese government. In 1905, faced with various pressures from the international market and the need to secure financial resources due to the cost of the Russo-Japanese War among others, the government enacted the Salt Monopoly Law. This law gave the government control over domestic salt production, pricing, and the improvement of production techniques. Later, in 1971, the government passed the Salt Industry Modernization Temporary Measures Act to modernize and streamline the salt industry. The act phased out older salt production methods, causing about 3,000 salt companies to disappear, leaving only seven exclusive operators in the country. As a result, Japan's traditional salt production methods, such as those that used salt fields, were effectively discontinued.

In 1997, regulatory laws governing salt production were finally revised, allowing for more competition and freedom in the industry. Mr. Inoue also had to wait until then to begin his salt production in earnest. When he did, he turned to the wisdom of the past. He apprenticed under a master versed in Japan's salt history and employed a production system that was first developed in 1953.

When I first saw Mr. Inoue's salt field, I was stunned by its beauty. Set against the sprawling sea of Yuya Bay, his multistory salt field is built from tiered layers of bamboo, which reminded me a little of a climbing structure in a children's playground. Using both the heat of the sun and the wind, the seawater is slowly concentrated with minerals as it trickles down the bamboo tiers. This process takes about one to two weeks, after which the concentrated saltwater must be boiled for several days.

Mr. Inoue considers the most important step in his process to be *tenchigaeshi* (天地返し), which literally translates to "turning heaven and earth." This ancient technique involves the act of flipping or turning the layers of salt.

"Because the salt crystals are white, you might think they stay the same from beginning to end, but that's not true. Four types of crystals form at different stages.

First calcium, second sodium, third potassium, and finally magnesium," Mr. Inoue explained. "If you package the salt without properly mixing them, you'll end up with an uneven product. By mixing the four salts, I'm trying to return the composition of the salt to the original balance of the sea."

The difference in the salt made by Mr. Inoue is immediately apparent. It's absolutely delicious. I get a surge of energy just by licking it. The flavor has depth, almost sweet—it's unparalleled. What's also remarkable about Mr. Inoue's salt, named Za You Zen, is that he offers a different variety for each of the four seasons in Yuya Bay. According to Mr. Inoue, the color, the shape of the crystals, and the amount of salt that can be extracted change depending on the season.

There is more seaweed in the ocean during the spring, so salt in this season has a taste reminiscent of seaweed. Salt in the summer has a strong *umami* flavor, as more nutrients flow out to the sea from the forest during the rainy season. Salt in autumn strikes a perfect balance of sodium and *umami*. Finally, the salt in winter is as pure as it can be, both in color and taste.

It's common knowledge that salt is an essential

component of our body. Meeting Mr. Inoue deepened my awareness of its importance to our well-being.

"Our bodies desire salt. We require it on a cellular level," he said. "Life on earth began in the sea, and the composition of the human body is similar to that of seawater. That's why it's important that the salt I make is as close as possible to the components of the sea. Natural sea salt can contain as many as seventy minerals that are naturally found in the sea. It can restore our health from the inside."

Mr. Inoue also shared with me what he loves most about his profession—it allows people to notice something fundamental: our connection to the ocean and the natural environment. Our relationship with nature is symbiotic. Protecting our environment is the same as protecting ourselves.

Salt may appear to be a simple, everyday seasoning, but it carries the memories of the sea, the forest, and the rain. Each grain holds a gift from the natural world, something to be savored with intention. For me, salt is more than a seasoning; it purifies both body and spirit, and nothing else feels quite as restorative.

Takigyo 滝行

The moment I stepped under the waterfall, I regretted it. Against the immense sound and pressure of the water, all I could do was close my eyes. And then there was the pain. The icy water pummeled me from the top of my head, making my knees buckle, threatening to take me down. "Did I have to do this?" I asked myself.

I was alone in the darkness, in the relentless pain. Yet somehow—don't ask me how—I remembered what I was supposed to do. I raised my shaky hands in front of my chest and brought my palms together in a prayer position. With the entire weight of the waterfall seemingly on my shoulders, I willed myself to straighten my spine.

My mind stopped panicking as I focused on my singular task: to stand alone beneath the cascade.

It was my client, an energetic business manager and a talented athlete skilled in a variety of sports, who had brought me to this moment in my life. She had only recently completed tidying her home using the KonMari Method. While tidying alongside her, I had the chance to get to know her well. Her many passions in life included a unique one that captivated me: meditating under a waterfall, a practice that she had been enjoying for over a decade. So when she casually asked me if I'd like to accompany her for her next trip, my curiosity got the better of me, and I heartily accepted her invitation.

I never expected the journey to the waterfall itself to be so arduous. I was woken up at my lodging at the crack of dawn and taken on a hike up a mountain path that felt endless. We eventually made it to a river where I found no bridges or pathways across. My client—many years my senior, mind you—began to wade into the knee-deep water without skipping a beat. I had no choice but to follow, and somehow we made it to the other shore. By the time we reached the small waterfall basin, I was exhausted.

In formal waterfall meditation, people wear traditional white robes worn by practitioners of Shinto or Buddhist rituals. In my case, we opted for the more casual attire of a white T-shirt and pants. Then, it was time to face the waterfall. This may sound obvious, but stepping beneath a waterfall isn't easy. You have to look for the right timing and slip in. I lost my nerve several times before I finally took the fateful step.

Though it felt like a terribly long time, in reality, it must have only been a few seconds. At first, I only heard the roar of the water, but soon I could hear my heartbeat, loud and clear. The pain, icicle-sharp and unbearable, soon subsided as a pleasant sensation of warmth began to rise from deep within me. I could feel the water, which had felt so dangerous and scary, penetrating deep into the pressure points of my head. My body soon grew numb while my mind became still and sharp, the powerful sound and pressure washing away every extraneous thought. I entered the most intense meditative state, one that I had never experienced before.

Later, as I was toweling off, I felt warm all over. Somehow, I had a smile on my face—I felt invigorated.

The Japanese word for waterfall ritual, *takigyo*

(滝行), combines the word *taki*, meaning waterfall, and *gyo*, as in *shugyo* or training. The term describes the long-held tradition of praying or chanting while standing underneath a waterfall, washing away both spiritual and moral impurity and deepening your connection to the divine. If you have visited a shrine in Japan, you might have noticed that one of the first rituals you partake in is to wash your hands with water using a wooden ladle called *hishaku* before you enter the sacred grounds of the shrine. Purification through water is an ancient and foundational concept in Japan. *Takigyo* as a spiritual training has been part of both Shinto and Buddhist traditions, and many waterfalls in Japan are considered sacred. In *Kojiki* (712 CE), one of the oldest historical texts in Japan, the god Izanagi performs *misogi*—ritual purification with water—after escaping the underworld.

Today, the image of someone praying or meditating beneath a waterfall might conjure a scene from an anime, manga, or film, as *takigyo* is often depicted as part of a hero's strenuous training in pursuit of a goal. For most Japanese people, *takigyo* is not a regular practice. The number of waterfalls where you can safely perform *takigyo* is limited, and the ritual can be dangerous if not done under the supervision of a trained guide. Even so, it seems more people today are practicing *takigyo* for a variety of reasons that aren't always religious. Modern practitioners of *takigyo* come from all walks of life—from business professionals looking to de-stress to spiritual seekers in search of meaning. This change reflects a broader trend in Japan and beyond, where ancient practices are being adapted to meet contemporary needs without losing their cultural essence.

Just last year, my husband, Takumi, also participated in *takigyo*. But I have to say he took things much further than my own experience many years ago. Takumi headed to the Tsubaki Grand Shrine in Suzuka City, Mie Prefecture, in November. The historic Shinto shrine is dedicated to Sarutahiko Okami, a powerful deity often associated with paths, guidance, and safe journeys. The shrine is especially popular among those seeking direction in life. It also organizes one of Japan's largest and most rigorous *takigyo* practices.

My husband decided to take the plunge with *takigyo* after listening to me talk passionately about its refreshing effect for years. He also happened to be invited to go along with a friend. But I have to say he possesses a much more adventurous spirit than I do. I don't think I could have gone through the ritual in the dead of winter in the middle of the night, which is exactly what he did. At around nine in the evening, Takumi and the rest of about 300 practitioners gathered together to hear a lecture by their guide, detailing the formal procedure of *takigyo* and its spiritual significance. Then, starting at ten, they spent an hour and a half taking turns stepping beneath the great waterfall. While women wore traditional white robes, men wore nothing but a loincloth!

"The cold was horrible," Takumi told me. "The kind of cold that feels like it's cutting through your skin. But every single person managed to go through with it."

"Why were they there?" I asked him. "What made them do it?"

Takumi shrugged. "All sorts of reasons," he said. "They want to organize what's on their minds, they hope to improve their lives, they want to let go of the guilt they've been carrying from the past."

"Wash everything away?"

"Yes. It's like stripping away unnecessary layers of yourself," Takumi said. "But what's fascinating is that everyone had such great expressions on their faces after they were done. I'll never forget that."

Like me, Takumi also noticed how his body grew strangely warm after a few minutes beneath the stinging downpour. He said he wasn't nearly as cold as he thought he would be when he finished. He could see the appeal of the ritual and why many people who experienced it once continued to incorporate it into their lifestyle.

Another fascinating thing about *takigyo* is how much it reminded me of tidying. I've always said my method of tidying should be a shock to the system. When I ask my clients to bring out every last item they own in a specific category—be it clothes, accessories, books, or sentimental items—they usually balk at the idea. A lot of us know deep down that we own so much more than what we see on the surface of our homes. As far as I'm concerned, the things that aren't being used in our lives are dormant, sleeping. I ask my clients to bring everything out in the open so that we can touch them and see them

> "Our true selves are far braver, more resilient, and more powerful than we often imagine."

for what they are and what they mean to us. This process is meant to create flow—a great rush of water, if you will—into corners of our homes that have remained stagnant for years.

Confronting a mountain of all the clothes you own is one way of confronting yourself—and that's not always easy to do. Yet once you push through the discomfort and start working through each piece, asking the same question over and over—does it spark joy for you?—a kind of silence falls around you and you enter a meditative state. With each thing you decide to let go or keep, you are stripping away the unnecessary clutter and restoring a truer version of yourself. There's a sacredness in creating space—both literally and metaphorically. When we clear our homes of items that no longer serve us, we also clear the mental noise that distracts us from our goals and values. I've watched people rediscover passions they had long forgotten, reconnect with loved ones, and step into new chapters of their lives with more clarity and confidence. Tidying is not just about folding or organizing—it's about aligning your environment with the life you want to lead.

It wasn't until I moved to the United States that I truly understood how a personal challenge reveals what you are made of. Surrounded by an unfamiliar culture and language, I really didn't know where to begin or what to do. All I knew was that I was determined to see how far I could take my philosophy of tidying—born in and inspired by Japan and its culture—beyond the confines of my native country. To say that I was nervous and fearful before going on a live taping of an American comedy talk show or tidying in homes of a country I didn't grow up in would be an understatement.

Every test of courage and determination, however, proved to me that my belief in the transformative nature of tidying is unshakeable. This belief was at the core of my identity and all that I needed to carry me through some of the toughest professional moments of my life. And this is exactly what happens when we go through something that scares us. We hear our own voice from deep within our hearts, telling us the answer to the questions *What do I want to do? Where should I go from here?*

Today, we live in a busy world where our sense of self can quickly be buried beneath clutter. Many of us are trying to free ourselves from what's unnecessary so that we can find our way back to our purer selves. That's what we are ultimately looking for from a purification ritual.

Purification doesn't always come through major challenges. I believe that even the quiet tears that fall unexpectedly in everyday life are a form of purification—like being gently washed by water.

I've experienced a "purification through tears" once in my past. It happened during the filming of my Netflix show. The shoot lasted about four months, during which my family stayed in Los Angeles and I was filming almost every day. Some days, I'd lead two tidying sessions with clients in their homes, then head to the studio to film clips of me giving organizing tips. I was always surrounded by a large crew.

One day, during a shoot at the home studio, I suddenly stopped in my tracks. At first, I was answering standard questions such as "What surprised you most during yesterday's session?" or "Any kitchen storage tips?" But as the questions began to dig deeper—"Why did you choose this career?" and "How ambitious are you about tidying the world?"—I was surprised to find myself at a complete loss for words.

What am I even doing here?

Once that thought entered my mind, before I knew it, tears started to fall. Three large cameras and about a dozen film crew were all staring intently at me. I suddenly felt waves of pressure closing in.

"I've always loved to tidy . . . that's all. It's very simple," I stammered. "I'm not used to talking in front of people."

My interpreter, Iida, carefully communicated my faltering words as an indescribable mood filled the studio. My feelings of insecurity, the frustration of not being able to find the right words, a fear of showing who I really was—with such feelings swirling within me, all I could do was let the tears flow.

After a long silence, one of the producers of the show kindly recognized my exhaustion and decided to finish the day early. Before we wrapped, she turned to me and said, "You are a lot stronger than you think. I truly believe that."

Her words in that moment became an undeniable turning point for me.

Those tears felt like a small ritual of purification— like a cleansing that I needed to accept myself. And after being purified, I rediscovered, even just a little, the strength to move forward again. The waterfall, tidying, and even the occasional tears—all of them have helped me return to my true self.

Another thing I've come to realize is that the producer's words—"You are a lot stronger than you think"—were absolutely correct. Our true selves are far braver, more resilient, and more powerful than we often imagine.

This is something I can say with confidence from my own experiences. Even when I was paralyzed by self-doubt, even when I cried, I kept getting back up and facing myself. And each time, little by little, I've come to believe in the strength that lies within me.

Even when we feel afraid, even when we shed tears—purifying ourselves, finding our balance, and living as our authentic selves is something anyone can do. I may have only stood beneath a waterfall once, but I've overcome piles of clothes many times and witnessed countless people transform in the process. And so can you.

CHAPTER 6

Harmonize

調和させる

Nihon Teien

日本庭園

If I were to be completely honest, when it comes to gardens, what I've always loved isn't Japanese gardens, but English gardens. I was deeply drawn to their brilliance from the time I was little. Rose petals wet with morning dew, lavender and chamomile blooming along a narrow path, white wooden benches and iron arches, birdbaths and tin watering cans. And quietly nestled somewhere, a small fairy statue. I adored that kind of world, scattered with tiny sparks of joy.

One of the reasons I came to long for English gardens was probably the influence of the stories I read as a child. The tea party in *Alice in Wonderland*, the flower-filled life in *Anne of Green Gables*—the scenes of characters letting their imaginations run free amidst the blooms made my heart flutter. To chat with someone under a rose arch, or sit on a white bench lost in thought . . . What a wonderfully romantic everyday life!

Yet my reality couldn't be further from my fantasy. I grew up in an apartment building, so I had no garden to speak of. Not only that, my room faced the interior hallway of the complex, with only a small window covered by bars that barely let in any natural light. A bright, colorful garden out of a storybook felt like nothing more than a distant dream. Hoping to get just a little closer to that ideal, I tried growing herbs in tiny pots in my room. But without enough sunlight, they kept withering again and again . . . I've got plenty of such pitiful little memories.

As I grew up and began to travel abroad, I always made a point to visit any English garden I heard about at my destination. In Los Angeles, I strolled through the gardens at the Huntington Library, and in London, I ventured into many gardens, starting with Hyde Park. Savoring the atmosphere in such places became one of the great joys of my travels. The fragrance of the flowers, the decorations, the seasonal shifts in color—all of it stirred my heart, awakening the dreams I had as a young girl.

Of course, it wasn't that I didn't know about the simple beauty of Japanese gardens. I had visited plenty of gardens during my domestic travels, from the gardens of Meiji Shrine in Tokyo to the Kenrokuen in Kanazawa. And yet, the radiance and decorative charm of English gardens held sway over my young mind.

As I went through life, however, a gradual change began to take place within me. As work became busier, my family grew, and daily life became more hectic, I found myself beginning to seek out "quiet" and "space." In the midst of a modern life constantly surrounded by noise and information, perhaps I unconsciously began to crave silence.

My encounter with Ryoan-ji Temple in Kyoto led me to truly appreciate the beauty of Japanese gardens. What brought me to this temple was a single remark— something said by the novelist Genki Kawamura, who coauthored my Japanese book, *Chatty Rooms*. One day, Genki-san told me, "If you're trying to spread the KonMari Method throughout the world, then you must visit Ryoan-ji." He was sure that I would be able to sense the connection between the temple and the message I'm trying to share with the world.

As if guided by his words, I made my way to Ryoan-ji. The temple, part of the Myōshin-ji school of the Rinzai branch of Zen Buddhism, is renowned worldwide for its dry landscape garden or *kare-sansui* (枯山水), composed chiefly of white gravel and fifteen carefully placed stones. At first glance, the garden appears plain—there's nothing decorative about it. And yet, I was rendered speechless by the profound meaning it seemed to hold within its silence.

The moment I stepped into the garden at Ryoan-ji, a mysterious stillness enveloped my heart. It was that gentle time in the morning when soft light filters into the garden, and the stones placed upon the white gravel stood solemnly, as if they had been cut off from the flow of time. There was hardly anyone around; only the sound of the wind and the chirping of the birds reached my ears. I slipped off my shoes, knelt on the veranda, and gazed out at the garden for a while.

The dry landscape garden at Ryoan-ji is arranged so that no matter which angle you view it from, at least one of the fifteen stones is always hidden from sight. In Eastern thought, the number fifteen symbolizes completeness—

like the full moon on the fifteenth night or the auspicious sum of numbers in the *Shichi-Go-San*, a traditional rite of passage celebration for children age three, five, and seven. And yet, in this garden, that "completeness" is deliberately made incomplete. There is beauty within its design of imperfection. It reflects the spirit of *wabi-sabi*—the Japanese sensibility that finds beauty in the naturally imperfect.

While *wabi* refers to the elegance of simplicity and *sabi* points to the depth that comes with the passage of time, both concepts value the constantly changing nature of the world. *Wabi-sabi* is deeply connected to Zen Buddhism, particularly the philosophy of *mujo* or impermanence. A Japanese garden is a living embodiment of the worldview that accepting the transient nature of things creates beauty.

At Ryoan-ji, what captured my heart the most was a stone water basin used for washing hands called a *tsukubai*. This unassuming vessel, placed in the corner of the garden, was carved with four *kanji* characters: 吾唯足知 (*ware tada taru wo shiru*), which translates to something like "I only know contentment." This refers to the Buddhist teaching of *chisoku*, the importance of knowing what is enough. Rather than feeling discontent over what is lacking, it teaches gratitude for what is already present, and to be at peace with things just as they are. This simple stone, nestled within the garden, manages to say so much about what's important in life.

As I sat looking out at the garden at Ryoan-ji, I recalled Genki-san's words: *You will be able to feel the garden's connection to the message you are trying to share with the world.* I suddenly knew exactly what he had meant.

The KonMari Method emphasizes the importance of reexamining your relationship with the things you own and asking what truly matters to you in the present. Tidying up isn't just about putting things in order—it's about confronting yourself and listening closely to your inner voice.

The Japanese garden is a space that begets harmony—it encourages us to contemplate the relationship between nature and humans. The rocks, the moss, the trees and the flowing water—all of them exist as if in dialogue with one another. Sitting in the stillness of the garden, I finally realized that the KonMari Method and Japanese gardens are tied to the same fundamental endeavor: to organize oneself in harmony with the surrounding world.

This experience awakened me to the charm of Japanese

gardens and I began visiting various gardens throughout Kyoto. Among them, the Hashin-tei in Komyo-in, a sub-temple of Tofuku-ji, left a lasting impression on me. A relatively unknown gem, the garden features seventy-five stones placed throughout its confines. At first glance, the stones seem shrouded in mystery, reminiscent of the Moai statues of Easter Island arranged at random. But when I looked more closely I started to notice a gentleness in their formation, as if they were small forest creatures that have gathered together to chat.

> "A Japanese garden is a living embodiment of the worldview that accepting the transient nature of things creates beauty."

My visit to the garden took place on an autumn evening, just as the fall foliage had reached its peak. The sun had set, and as the garden grew dim, soft lights began to illuminate each stone and mossy area. The red and orange-hued maple leaves, illuminated from below, seemed to float against the darkness—as if the entire garden were quietly breathing.

One of the key techniques in Japanese garden design

is *shakkei* (借景), meaning borrowed scenery. Originating from Chinese garden culture developed during the Song dynasty, *shakkei* involves incorporating the distant natural landscapes behind the garden, such as mountains, forests, and the sky, into the design of the garden itself. The technique captures the surrounding nature as it is—alive and untamed—and renders it part of the garden, bringing a sense of depth and expansiveness to the space. Notable examples include Enko-ji Temple in Kyoto and the Katsura Imperial Villa, and they are a powerful reflection of the Japanese aesthetic of humans harmonizing with nature.

Gazing at the illuminated Hashin-tei garden, I was moved by its majestic sense of life. The stones seemed almost alive, and I felt as if I were witnessing a cutout of a natural landscape, frozen in time. I could see that the stones, seemingly placed at random, were in fact meticulously positioned, revealing the presence of a uniquely Japanese aesthetic sensibility.

Speaking of stones and Japanese gardens, I'm reminded of another person who left an indelible impression on me.

"Until recently, I was a stone." This was what Mr. Makoto Kitazawa, a veteran gardener, told me the first time I met him. Although he uttered the remark wryly, I remember his expression was quite serious. I instinctively knew at that moment that here was a person who knew how to commune with stones.

Mr. Kitazawa grew up in an area within Kyoto that is particularly rich in nature, close to the famous Kinkaku-ji Temple and Arashiyama district. He explained to me that his sensibility developed from an early age in a boundary between the human and natural worlds. As the third-generation owner of the family business, Kitazawa Landscaping, Mr. Kitazawa's words are filled with overwhelming respect for and deep affection toward nature.

"Stones are so much more than a material," he said. "I almost think they have a consciousness. For me, the moment in gardening that sparks the most joy is when I place a stone. It's the best when I can place one without thinking about it. My own consciousness doesn't intervene in the moment, and I'm moved solely by the atmosphere of the place, or something like a deity. It's in such a moment, which hovers between consciousness and unconsciousness, that the most precise things are created."

Mr. Kitazawa told me that his favorite stone in the

world is the one that floats in the sea off the Echizen Coast in Fukui Prefecture.

"When I first saw that stone, I had such a profound feeling that it brought me to tears. For the first time, I felt as though the stone, just like a human, had its own consciousness."

Talking to him, I could see that what holds a Japanese garden together is not only structural beauty but a profound spirituality. Many of Mr. Kitazawa's gardens are designed so that their beauty can be sustained even with maintenance only once or twice a year. He achieves this by respecting the natural shape of the trees without resorting to excessive pruning, which makes them easier to manage.

"People sometimes add brilliance to a garden in imaginative ways, such as installing a fountain. It's one way of designing a space in dialogue with nature," he said. "In contrast, Japanese gardens focus on drawing out the beauty that nature already possesses. We begin by humbling ourselves before its overwhelming, incomparable beauty. I believe that creating a beautiful space is a kind of prayer— a way for us as humans to seek guidance from nature."

The act of creating beauty versus the act of bringing out inherent beauty—this contrast reveals not only cultural differences but differing attitudes toward nature. A Japanese garden is an art form that values harmony, humility, and a dialogue with our subconscious.

"Long ago, our daily lives were steeped in a deeper sense of gratitude toward nature and a desire to live in harmony with it. A Japanese garden is an embodiment of such sensibilities," Mr. Kitazawa said. "We tend to forget this, but I see more and more young people and people from overseas being drawn to it. When we have enough materially, we begin to seek spiritual fulfillment."

These days, Mr. Kitazawa works on garden projects far away from home, including the U.S. and the U.A.E. Through his experiences abroad, he's come to understand why Japanese gardens are being sought after around the world.

Today, Japanese gardens can be found all over the world, with more than 300 said to exist in the United States alone. Notable examples include the Portland Japanese Garden in Oregon and the Japanese Garden within the Brooklyn Botanic Garden in New York. These gardens are appreciated not only as beautiful spaces, but also as places where people can experience silence and harmony and be at one with nature.

The KonMari Method has also spread across the world, with many people seeking to reclaim quiet moments of self-reflection through tidying and the search for their own spark of joy. Perhaps this stems from the same longing we feel toward Japanese gardens— a desire to connect with nature and return to our most fundamental values. In organizing the external world to better understand our inner one, we find a shared pursuit that transcends national boundaries.

After my conversation with Mr. Kitazawa, I suddenly unlocked a distant memory. My grandparents had a house in Miyazaki Prefecture, and in its yard was a classic Japanese garden. There was a pond with koi swimming in it, a small waterfall, and a stone bridge.

I have memories of simply standing still in that garden as a little girl. I wasn't thinking about anything in particular. I was merely staring at the stones, feeling the wind, sensing the change in the seasons. I was free of self-consciousness, merely content to be with myself and the nature that surrounded me. But now, looking back, I realize that this was a visceral experience that a Japanese garden is meant to offer—a time to exist in stillness with nature. It was such a quiet memory that it must have become buried in my mind.

If I were to visit that garden again now, I feel I would be able to appreciate more deeply the sounds and the atmosphere, the expressions of the stones, the scent of the grass. Standing in that space, I would once again reaffirm my connection with the world—just as I did back then, but with entirely different eyes and years of experiences beyond the wildest imagination of my younger self.

In the end, to place oneself in the stillness is to let go—to feel the empty space, to surrender yourself to it, and become one with the wind and light. In such a place, harmony isn't about neatly organizing every detail, but rather allowing each element to exist as is, with all its idiosyncrasies and variety.

The experience of tranquility, found in a Japanese garden, connects our hearts to Japan and to our most authentic selves, no matter where we are or where we come from. It feels like a gentle letter from Japan, addressed with care to us all.

Jinja 神社

When I was eighteen years old, I worked as a shrine maiden near my childhood home in Japan. Shrine maidens, known as *miko* (巫女), perform various tasks at Shinto shrines. I wore a crisp white kimono top and scarlet red pleated trousers, and was stationed near the front of the shrine where we issued talismans. The talismans available at Shinto shrines are typically wooden prayer tablets or small protective charms called *omamori,* which are wrapped in beautifully embroidered cloth tied with a string. Each talisman is blessed by the shrine's priests and is meant for a specific purpose.

As I distributed these talismans to visitors, I became more aware of the common anxieties and hopes that we all share as human beings: seeking protection from illnesses or accidents, blessings for romantic relationships, academic success, safety while traveling, and prosperity.

My fondness for shrines developed at an even younger age. In elementary school, I attended a cram school, Japan's version of test prep centers, where I studied for my junior high school entrance exam. The Kanda Myojin Shrine, one of the oldest and most revered Shinto shrines in Tokyo, stood right behind my cram school. I was too young to give much thought to religion, but the shrine was a constant, comforting presence in those days. It soon became a ritual for me to visit Kanda Myojin and pray that I would be accepted into the school of my choice. Expressing my worries and hopes in this way must have given me courage, allowing me to stay focused and positive throughout the application process. When I was finally accepted into the school I had hoped for, I went straight back to the shrine to say thank you.

I was in high school when I found a notice in front of a local shrine near my home, saying they were looking for shrine maidens to help with the busy New Year's holiday season. On January 1st and in the days following, many Japanese people flock to their favorite shrines to pray for good health and fortune in the year ahead. In addition to receiving charms and prayer tablets, many also participate in fortune-telling and purification rituals. I thought it would be the perfect job for me and signed up immediately.

Years later, I never could have expected that writing about my experience as a young shrine maiden would spark so many questions from readers and the media abroad. Journalists would ask: Was I deeply religious? Do I practice Shinto every day? What kind of connection does the KonMari Method of tidying have to Shinto? These questions stumped me. Even though I've always liked shrines, I never considered myself belonging to a particular religion. When it comes to my relationship with shrines, it's not so much about defining a singular religion as it is about achieving internal harmony. In Japan, it's common for people to celebrate Christmas at home, have their wedding in a church, and visit a shrine every New Year to pray for health and prosperity. I believe that freely incorporating aspects of different cultures that improve our well-being is a defining feature of the Japanese sensibility and lifestyle.

When you grow up in Japan, shrines become a familiar

part of your surroundings. As children, we visit shrines on school trips, and when we travel around the country, local shrines are often included in the itinerary. There are two main reasons for my personal affinity with shrines. First, as a professional tidying consultant, I can't think of a more inspiring place. At many shrines, the grounds are regularly swept clean with care, arranged as if not even a single fallen leaf or stone is out of place. Every architectural detail seems to be thoughtfully established with a purpose and meaning—you could say a shrine has a strong sense of itself.

If you've ever visited Japan, you might have experienced walking into a shrine in the middle of a busy urban neighborhood. Despite the hustle and bustle surrounding it, you can immediately feel the hushed, sacred atmosphere as soon as you step inside. A comfortable yet refreshing coolness surrounds you, bringing with it a sense of tranquility that I love so much. Perhaps shrines are the ultimate inspiration for my tidying philosophy.

Second, I appreciate the way a shrine affects my mind and spirit. When I find myself enveloped in that quiet calmness, it gives me an opportunity to check in with myself. I find myself answering questions that weigh heavily on my mind—*What are the troubles I'm facing right now? How should I proceed?*—with more honesty and integrity. A visit to a shrine allows me to set my goals and intentions. When I feel overwhelmed by the demands of daily life, I walk up the *sando* road leading straight to the main hall of the shrine and find my way again. I offer a prayer, and for a brief moment, I remember what it feels like to be in harmony with myself.

The phrase *Nirei nihakushu ichirei* (二礼二拍手一礼), which translates to "two bows, two claps, and one bow," describes the sequence of actions performed when paying respects at a shrine. Upon reaching the main hall, you first stand with your heels together. Then, maintaining good posture throughout, you bow twice slowly, bending from the hips at a ninety-degree angle.

The two bows are followed by two claps. Sound plays an important role in Shinto purification rituals. When performed properly and with intention, a simple clap can purify the surrounding energy and space. If you ever hear a seasoned Shinto priest clap, you might be amazed by the bright, resonant sound they can produce with just their hands. The sequence concludes with a final deep bow.

Throughout this book, you may have noticed that I

mention things and ideas that inspire me to straighten my back. In our lives filled with screens, how often do we find ourselves with aching backs from poor posture? A shrine is a place that seems to compel every visitor to stand taller. When you perform the "two bows, two claps, and one bow" sequence with enough energy and commitment, it feels as though your entire body has lengthened; it brings so much awareness to your body.

The irony of our modern existence is that, despite living in a world full of noises and images, we rarely get the chance to use all five of our senses to truly experience something. A shrine is one of the few places that offers this rare opportunity. You taste the cold, cleansing water as you rinse your mouth at the water basin before entering the shrine. You hear the bell ring as you shake it before the altar. You breathe in the scent of incense in the air. You see history preserved in the ancient, sacred cedar or oak

> "In our lives filled with screens, how often do we find ourselves with aching backs from poor posture? A shrine is a place that seems to compel every visitor to stand taller."

tree just behind the main hall, and you marvel at all that it has witnessed over the years. A simple stroll through the shrine never fails to align my body and spirit.

To bring the inspiration from a shrine into everyday life, I keep the small altar I mentioned earlier, a *kamidana,* in my home. The idea behind this altar is to create my own tiny shrine within the house. It's not uncommon to have a home altar in Japan. Recently, in addition to traditional *kamidana,* simple and stylish ones that blend with contemporary interior design have also been introduced, and this is the type we use in our home. Many households decorate their altars with branches of *sasaki* (Japanese cleyera), which is considered a sacred tree in Shinto. An evergreen broadleaf tree, *sasaki* has played an important role in Shinto rituals. Regardless of religious connotations, I believe it's a good idea to have a corner in your home that helps you recharge your energy. Distractions are everywhere in our world today, and it's too easy to lose track of who we are and who we aspire to be. Waves of change can hit us at any moment.

In Shinto, there is sanctity in ritual and repetition, whether it's sweeping the grounds of the shrine every morning or conducting a seasonal ceremony on the same day of the same month each year. The simple, unchanging ritual I perform every morning before my little altar helps bring harmony to my day, no matter what new challenges I face. This sense of consistency could be one reason why Japanese people feel comforted by shrines. Shinto is the indigenous faith of Japan, and the shrines, the grounds they are built on, and the customs and rites performed within them have stood the test of time, remaining unchanged for hundreds of years. Even if people only visit the shrine a few times or even once a year, they expect their neighborhood shrines to stay the same.

Another notable aspect of shrines is their accessibility. The *torii* gate, which you walk under, marks the entrance to the sacred ground of a shrine. There are no heavy doors to unlock or push open. An internal shift in consciousness naturally occurs when you step into a shrine. Yet, the architectural details of a Shinto shrine, from the stone guardian lion-dogs to the subdued, calming colors of its natural materials, somehow blend seamlessly into its surroundings. A neighborhood in Japan would feel incomplete without a shrine.

In the early ninth century, when some of the first shrines were built in Japan, they did not have the main hall we see today. In ancient times, people prayed and performed rites before mountains, large trees, and even boulders—nature itself was considered sacred. This was the origin of shrines and the belief that *"yaoyorozu-no-kami"* (eight million deities) reside in all of nature. If you venture into the countryside of Japan, you will notice miniature shrines erected by the side of the road, along rice paddies, or in gardens. The Omiwa Shrine in Nara worships the whole of Mount Miwa behind it as a deity. Over time, these Shinto beliefs diffused into the everyday culture and customs of the Japanese people.

Japanese fishermen pray to the deity of the sea for safety, farmers honor the deity of the mountain for a bountiful harvest, and we even perform rites for good fortune and protection before building a house or starting a film shoot. There is a sensibility among Japanese people that we should strive to live in harmony with everything around us. The relationship we have with our surroundings isn't hierarchical. There is a deity—or soul, if you prefer—that resides in something as vast as a mountain and something as small as a cooking pot, both deserving our equal respect and care.

I find this belief to be more elemental than religious.

When I first begin tidying in a new home, I introduce myself to the house, asking for its help in the process. When I decide to let go of something, I do so with gratitude, expressing thanks out loud. When I come home after a busy day, I fold or hang my clothes with extra care, knowing they have served me well. Such old habits of mine often attracted many questions and sometimes some puzzled looks when I did them outside Japan. Perhaps my appreciation for shrines can explain the heart behind my practice.

Speaking of habits, one of the first things I do when I move into a new neighborhood in Japan is call the local administrative organ of the *Jinja-cho*, or shrine agency. If you provide your address, the agency can tell you which shrine has jurisdiction over your neighborhood. Everywhere in Japan, there is a guardian deity called *Ujigami* that is believed to watch over the community. This is why I always make sure to visit my local shrine and introduce myself to the deity before I begin a new chapter in a new place. But there's nothing quite like a shrine with which you form a personal connection.

Each Shinto shrine has a specialty or focus, such as academic success or familial relationships. For example, the Kanda Myojin shrine, popular with people seeking business success, is known for triumph over challenges.

Another shrine that I feel a special kinship with is Ise Jingu, located in Mie Prefecture along the Pacific coast. Ise Jingu is considered the spiritual heart of Shinto, consisting of 125 shrines centered around the main inner sanctuary called *Naiku*. About 2,000 years ago, *Amaterasu-Omikami*, the deity of the imperial family and a revered guardian of Japan, was enshrined in Ise Jingu. What makes this shrine truly unique in the world is that the wooden structure of the shrine is torn down and rebuilt every twenty years as part of a ceremony. The tradition helps preserve the original architecture and also ensures that traditional technologies and craftsmanship of ancient Japan are passed down to the next generation. Attracted by the shrine's incredible history and the more than 1,500 rituals conducted throughout the year, millions of people visit it each year.

When I visit Ise Jingu, I try to do so with a receptive, open heart, asking it to guide me into whatever role I should take on next. The inner sanctuary of Ise Jingu is located within a sacred mountain. Just walking through its *torii* gate makes you feel as if you've passed into a different world, a spiritual realm. It's a shrine that has been carefully maintained through time and prayer.

After a visit to Ise Jingu, I feel purified and refreshed. Curiously enough, soon after the visit, a new project or an opportunity to go overseas will often come my way, opening me to a direction I hadn't considered before.

When I travel abroad, I love finding spaces that shift my thinking and open me to new ways of looking at the world. I feel that a shrine is one of those places. There are shrines that can give you something you need, just as there are shrines that help you let go of something. Each shrine offers something different, and I believe a person is led to a specific shrine when they need it most.

All shrines are meant to bring you back to yourself, to a more harmonious way of life. When you visit a shrine, there's so much to take in, from its history to its architecture. But I hope you'll also remember to let it give you that quiet moment of peace, which has grown so scarce these days. You might even find a message that you didn't even know you needed, emerging from deep inside of you.

Kotoba 言葉

"Choose only the things that spark joy for you" translates in Japanese to *Tokimekumono wo erabimasho* (ときめくものを選びましょう). In my mind, I know that the two sentences say the same thing, but when I say them out loud, I can't help but feel that the English version comes out stronger.

In Japanese, the subject of the sentence is the inanimate *tokimekumono*, or "the things that spark joy," whereas in English, the sentence becomes a clear command given by one person to another. The sentence starts off with the word "choose," which puts emphasis on the action that I'm asking you to do. The Japanese version is more of a gentle suggestion that communicates the general importance of choosing what sparks joy.

Even the phrase "things that spark joy" doesn't have the same ring as the Japanese *tokimekumono*. The two say the same thing, but there are so many differences, from the sound to the movement of my mouth when I say the words. It took some time for me to get used to this English version. I even think that when I give my tidying lessons in English, I become a different person, a different personality, from who I am in my native country.

As a non-native English speaker, I'm conscious of the subtle physical changes I experience when I speak English. I have to open my mouth wider and speak clearly from my diaphragm. I use different muscles. I feel sensations I do not feel when I'm speaking in my native tongue.

When I first moved to the U.S., I was barely able to communicate in English. It wasn't so much that I got the vocabulary or the phrasing wrong: I spoke too quietly. I'm rather soft-spoken, even when compared to most Japanese people, but in America, I soon realized that people couldn't hear me, let alone understand what I was trying to communicate.

The inevitable "What?!" or "What did you say?" that came in response to my English made me shrink. I would hesitate, unsure if I said something wrong or did something to prevent me from being understood. I cannot tell you the number of times I would get the wrong order when I asked for something at a café or a restaurant. I have no idea what part of my pronunciation or word choice led to me receiving a turkey sandwich when I asked for a simple morning toast!

I feel that English is a language that requires a certain amount of confidence to speak. It's a language that allows you to voice your opinion boldly, which isn't my strong suit (though I'm working on it!). When I speak in Japanese, I feel I can get away with speaking softly.

Speaking in your native language often feels natural and effortless, but to my ear, there's something especially soothing and gentle about the sound of Japanese. This may be because many Japanese words end in vowels, giving the language a smooth, melodic quality. I once read that natural sounds—like wind, ocean waves, the chirping of insects, and birdcalls—tend to have vowel-like qualities to the human ear, which might help explain the calming effect. If language reflects the values of a culture, then the softness and roundness of Japanese may mirror the society's emphasis on harmony—not just among people, but also with nature. As an island nation, Japan has long valued unity, cooperation, and balance, and it's easy to imagine that this cultural mindset has influenced the way the language has evolved.

When I go to the bookstore in Japan, I'm always astonished at the number of reference books and manuals on writing letters and emails, especially for professional purposes. An essential part of Japanese communication is *keigo*, the system of honorific language used to show respect, humility, or politeness that also reflects social hierarchy, such as age and experience. *Keigo* can be challenging even for native speakers, but you can't quite handle formal or professional situations in Japan without it.

Just like how we change outfits depending on the occasion, Japanese language adapts to the situation. We select different words for a business meeting, a casual get-together with friends of the same age, or a visit with the in-laws. The reason so many people strive to master the etiquette of the Japanese language is because it holds the key to upholding the values of social harmony.

For example, when writing a business email, instead of launching right into the main topic, it's often advised to write a few opening remarks about the season or something about nature that you've noticed. At the height of summer, you might comment on the chorus of cicadas you heard while commuting to work. At the beginning of fall, when the weather is just starting to turn brisk, you might start off a letter by writing "The footsteps of autumn are drawing near." Such phrases aren't meant to be empty words; they convey a spirit of goodwill that gives depth and color to what could otherwise be an impersonal transaction. While technological advancement has greatly simplified our digital exchanges, especially in certain industries, the intention behind such greetings remains at the heart of the Japanese way of communication.

Another common piece of advice that Japanese people give when trying to achieve harmonious communication is to ensure that your actions or words "don't cause any corners to stick out" or *kado ga tatanai* (かどがたたない). I find the idiom useful in that it helps you remember to avoid any insensitive words or a brusque attitude that has the potential to be a "sharp corner" that causes friction in your interaction with others. Yet sharp corners are a part of life. We don't always see eye to eye with others.

You might feel slighted or offended and feel the urge to hit back with some harsh words. So what helps when you bump into such sharp corners?

Cushion kotoba or "cushion words" in Japanese are words and phrases used at the beginning of a sentence to make a request, refusal, opinion, or correction sound more indirect and nonconfrontational. They cushion what you're about to say so it doesn't come off as too direct. One of the most quintessential and versatile examples of a Japanese cushion word is *osore irimasuga* (恐れ入りますが), which translates roughly in English to "I'm sorry to bother you, but . . ."

> "In Japan, *ikigai* is often described as the thing that inspires you to get out of bed each morning — the quiet motivation that fills your life with meaning and purpose."

Saying *osore irimasuga* before asking someone for help or apologizing for a delay naturally makes the receiver more open to accepting it, and it gives the speaker a softer, more considerate impression.

In our rush to communicate and get to the bottom of things, we might consider such practices old-fashioned or evasive. But cushion words are meant to give a moment of reflection, some space for us to be more conscious of our words and delivery. A cushion word might just be what you need to take a pause and cool down when emotions get heated.

Another aspect of the Japanese language is that it's entirely possible to carry on an entire conversation without stating an "I" or a "you." When I began speaking more in English, I found the emphasis placed on the subject and the object of the sentence both refreshing and difficult. Whether you are speaking in the first, second, or third person, there's never any confusion about who the subject is and to whom you are speaking. Compared to English, Japanese feels intentionally ambiguous.

Take, for instance, the expression *arigato* or "thank you" in Japanese. When you say "thank you" to a person, there's never any confusion about the direction of the message—it's moving from "me" to "you." Or when you say "I appreciate it," the "it" makes it clear what you are thankful for. Yet when I say *arigato*, both the subject and the object of the message are ambiguous. Once *arigato* is uttered, it's as if the message floats lightly into the air like a bubble and then disappears into the atmosphere.

It's quite a strange sensation, one that I've never noticed when I used to speak only in Japanese.

I did a little research and learned that *arigato* derives from *arigatai*, the word that means "grateful" or "thankful" and is used to express a feeling of deep appreciation or gratitude for something that's not easily taken for granted. The *kanji* characters for this word, 有難い, literally mean "hard to exist" or "rare" (有 = to have, 難 = difficult). So when you say *arigato*, what you're actually saying is that what you are thankful for is "impossible," implying that something is so rare or precious in this world that it's worthy of gratitude.

In *arigato*, unlike "thank you," there is no "I," "you," or even "gratitude"; the word merely states the impossibility of the situation at hand. While English words of appreciation are often attributed to a specific person, *arigato* is a comment upon the stark reality of the world—a harsh world where good things seem rare and impossible, which makes it all the more joyous when a kind gesture or a beautiful event *does* take place.

Of course, such ambiguity in the Japanese language does have its limitations. While things have improved markedly in the last decade, it used to be fairly common for business negotiations in Japan to also be shrouded in ambiguity. I remember that fifteen years ago, when I first began writing books, it was common practice for publishers to mention contracts only after the book had been nearly finished and the publishing date had been set. Talks of fees and percentages would occur after the fact. The assumption that things would work out smoothly because of mutual trust and belief in social harmony is all well and good when the business relationship is stable, but it could lead to frustration and misunderstanding otherwise.

This might sound obvious to most people in the West, but I feel that I learned the importance of making your intentions and positions clear through a contract only by working outside of Japan. The more indirect and vague approach of the Japanese takes the feelings of other people into consideration, but demarcating a clear boundary between yourself and others is also necessary for a healthy working relationship.

My experience of releasing my book overseas has also taught me to boldly reclaim my subjectivity—the "I" in my sentences—which probably doesn't come very naturally to most Japanese people. While trying to promote my books and share my tidying method with the media, I would often run into interviews where the journalist would excitedly say, "So, tell me about your success!" This request never failed to make me nervous in those early days.

My stance is that whatever success my book managed to achieve is due to the inherent wonder of tidying. So it feels rather strange to me to frame the popularity of tidying as "my personal success." When the attention began to shift toward me and my personal life, it made me feel self-conscious in ways that I had never experienced before.

During interviews, I've often felt that I'm not very good at talking about myself. I can talk for hours about the techniques of tidying, what it means for something to spark joy, and how the things we consciously choose to keep can change our mindset and the way we live. But I've now spent a decade working overseas, and I think I'm getting the hang of responding to personal questions. If anything, such questions have helped me appreciate the importance of having my own views and opinions and voicing them with confidence.

I've certainly come a long way from never getting the item I ordered at a café to speaking on huge stages at conferences and events before a live audience. There's no hiding from myself when giving a lecture or a presentation in English—you never feel quite as naked and alone as when you are standing alone on a stage. Whenever I have an opportunity to go onstage, I still feel a little untethered, as if I'm floating away from my body, but I've learned to embrace my subjectivity for the most part. I only have to hope that my voice will be loud enough to carry my message across.

Still, I will always see myself as a conduit for the magic of tidying. I feel like I can perform better when there's not much of an "I" involved. To inspire people to live a life that sparks joy for them through tidying—this is my role and purpose in life, or what the Japanese call *ikigai*.

I've recently learned that the Japanese word *ikigai* has become popular in the U.S. *Ikigai* is a small word with a big meaning, most often translated as "a reason for being." It's about finding the intersection of what you love to do, what you're good at, what society needs, and what you can be paid for. But I feel that sometimes the most important aspect of *ikigai* becomes a bit lost in translation.

In Japan, *ikigai* is often described as the thing that inspires you to get out of bed each morning—the quiet motivation that fills your life with meaning and purpose. It's more than a goal or aspiration; it's the feeling that your existence matters. It's what makes you feel truly alive.

My *ikigai* doesn't revolve around financial success or career ambition. It goes deeper than that. I find my *ikigai* in helping others rediscover joy through the simple, powerful act of tidying. When I guide someone to choose what they truly cherish, to let go of what no longer serves them, and to begin living a life surrounded only by things that spark joy, I feel most fulfilled. To witness that transformation is my greatest reward. In those moments, I feel it in my bones: yes, my life is worth living.

While each of us has our own passions and paths, I believe many of us are seeking something similar: a sense of connection to something greater than ourselves. No matter our background, we long to feel in harmony with the world around us. We want to belong. We want to contribute. Learning another language has deepened this awareness for me.

It's said that the Japanese term for language or words, *kotoba* (言葉), is derived from *koto* (こと), meaning thought or event, and *ha* (は or 端), meaning edge or periphery. When you think of words as something that suddenly emerges from the depth of your heart and mind, it seems that words are not just sounds, but rather a part of ourselves. And through such words we began to consider how we connect with others and what kind of bridges we are trying to build.

In a world increasingly filtered through screens, it's easy to forget that on the other side of every message is a person. Am I getting across what I want to say? Am I being sufficiently heard? Of course, these are important questions to consider when trying to communicate with others. But beyond that, we should also ask: How do my words affect others? Do my words come from a place of kindness and love?

Language carries our values. Our words shape our relationships, and, ultimately, our shared reality. In a time when so much feels uncertain, I believe it's more important than ever to speak with intention, to write with kindness. All this is to say that I'm thinking about you, dear reader, as I write these words, hoping that, despite the distance and time between us, they will connect us.

Ma 間

During the filming of my Netflix show, *Tidying Up with Marie Kondo*, a similar scene occurred time and again. While sorting through belongings in their homes, clients would stop suddenly, holding up a sentimental item. They would caress it, set it down, then pick it up again, unable to decide whether to keep or discard it. They agonized over their decision for a long time. Whenever this happened, I would sit across from them, waiting silently. I never interrupted. From the corner of my eye, I noticed producers fidgeting behind the camera. The lighting technician and the boom operator would exchange uneasy glances. Some of the crew members may have even suppressed yawns.

Of course, I understand that the job of a reality TV host is to talk. The camera is rolling—we're in action! I could offer numerous suggestions when my clients struggle with tidying—*How does this item make you feel? What are you thinking about right now?*—but I believe in giving them time and space to reflect and process their emotions on their own. This approach also allows me to develop empathy and sensitivity to my clients' needs. I incorporate stillness and silence in other aspects of my tidying method as well. When first entering a client's home, I spend a few minutes silently introducing myself to the space, asking for its support in the tidying process. I also enjoy sitting quietly with clients when I teach them how to fold clothes. I'm perfectly at ease sitting in silence with someone I've just met while we fold each item from a big pile. Of course, I do engage in intimate conversations with clients at times, but I value the time we spend without talking just as much.

I've also been told that my lectures and seminars often include moments of silence. I sometimes need to pause to gather my thoughts. Speaking before a large audience is nerve-racking—especially when doing so in a second language! But even when standing on the grandest stage, I frequently find myself looking around the room and absorbing its energy. These pauses I take and the spaces I maintain between both things and people are an important part of my approach to work and life. Japanese has a unique word for such intervals: *ma* (間).

The *kanji* character for *ma* combines the symbols of gate (門) and sun (日). The word evokes an image of sunlight filtering through the empty space of a doorway. *Ma*, as an intrinsic Japanese sensibility, is evident in its many uses in common expressions and phrases. Broadly speaking, there are three types of *ma*: temporal (the *kanji* character for time is *jikan* 時間), spatial (the *kanji* character for space is *kukan* 空間), and abstract (the *kanji* character for human is *ningen* 人間 and society is *seken* 世間). *Ma* also appears in words that judge quality: *ma-ni-au* (間に合う) indicates something that is satisfactory or on time; someone who can't get in rhythm or adapt to the flow of their surroundings is called a *ma-nuke* (間抜け), which literally translates to someone lacking *ma*.

It might be a difficult concept to grasp at first, but once you train yourself to see *ma*, you'll notice it everywhere in Japan. The countless examples of *ma* in classical Japanese art prove that the Japanese people have spent centuries thinking about the concept. It's not an exaggeration to say that *ma* forms the foundation of Japanese culture and lifestyle. For instance, traditional Japanese architecture lacked clearly defined "rooms." Instead, spaces vaguely set apart by pillars in the room were called *ma*. *Tokonoma* (床の間) means alcove and *kyakuma* (客間) means guest room. This practice of attributing meaning to empty space significantly impacted Japanese aesthetics. *Shoji* screens, another common feature in a traditional Japanese room, are made of thin, translucent paper. These dividers allow light and wind to pass through, creating a space neither completely outside nor inside. Japanese appreciation for changing seasons could be attributed to living in such spaces that literally existed between nature and the home.

From tea ceremony to calligraphy, *ma* is at the heart of traditional Japanese art and culture. I will never forget my first lesson in *kado* or Japanese flower arrangement. The instructor explained that the spaces in between the flowers are just as important as the flowers themselves. How will you shape the contours of the gap between two branches or the margins around the blossoms? How much of the wall behind the arrangement do you want to show?

A Japanese flower arrangement may include merely a stem or two of flowers or leaves, but by altering the angle or the way the stems intersect, the whole space in which the arrangement exists transforms.

Nihonga, a traditional Japanese painting style using *sumi* ink on paper, often includes expansive margins. Whatever is drawn with ink exists to emphasize the white emptiness that surrounds it. A similar effect is found in Japanese rock gardens. While Western gardens typically feel lush and complete, Japanese rock gardens are sparse, treating space differently. They convey more than what is visible by intentionally drawing attention to what's absent. Another dynamic example of *ma* is seen in *kabuki* theater. During pivotal scenes, when a character's emotions peak, the actor strikes a powerful pose and momentarily freezes. This technique, called *mie*, meaning "appearance" or "visible" in Japanese, highlights key narrative moments. All movement onstage—the actors, music, and sound effects—stops in time with *mie*. As one of *kabuki*'s most captivating conventions, *mie* comes in various forms. An actor may turn his head, extend his hands, step forward, or stamp his foot. If portraying anger, he may cross his eyes and fix a withering glare at the audience. Regardless of style, this technique powerfully illustrates the shared experience of *ma* between performers and audience.

The concept of *ma* also reminds me of the Japanese filmmaker Yasujiro Ozu. Ozu, one of the legendary directors of Japanese cinema, began working in silent film and continued through the postwar era. He is renowned for his *shomin-geki*, or modern family dramas, which explore the generational divides between parents and children. Dialogue in Ozu's films is understated, and interactions between his characters are subtle and restrained. His camerawork is also quietly observant, often lingering on empty shots of rooms and landscapes long after the characters have departed. To me, Ozu's films seem to breathe more gently, with frequent moments of *ma* in between. Perhaps that's why his work feels distinctively Japanese.

In *Tokyo Story*, Ozu's masterpiece from 1953, an aging couple from the countryside visits Tokyo to see their grown children. In the big city, we witness the couple's estrangement from their children, who are too absorbed in their busy lives to view their parents as anything more than a burden. Only when one parent falls ill does the entire family come together in the same room. In a scene when the family gathers around the deathbed, Ozu makes a curious directorial move. He cuts away from the moment of life and death, instead showing an extended series of images— boats, train tracks, and the sea, most devoid of people. When we return to the family, the parent has passed, and the children are now weeping. I often wonder what Ozu intended to convey with these sequences. Are the shots meant to represent memorable places the family visited together? Ozu uses similar images of empty landscapes in many of his films, and critics have passionately speculated on their meanings. To me, these sequences are Ozu's way of inserting *ma* into an important scene. By momentarily removing us from the action, Ozu allows us to fully absorb the emotional weight of what the characters are going through. It's as if he places a respectful distance between the audience and the characters, making the pathos of the scene even more poignant by not showing their emotions directly.

> "Once you train yourself to see *ma*, you'll notice it everywhere in Japan."

Today, film enthusiasts still visit Ozu's grave in Japan. His gravestone is marked by a single *kanji* character:

mu (無), meaning nothingness. Another way to understand *ma* is through its connection to *mu*. In Zen philosophy, appreciating the empty spaces in both space and time is thought to bring harmony and serenity to the heart. *Mu* signifies abundance—nothingness filled with limitless potential. *Ma* is the force that acts upon this nothingness. It breathes life into the nothingness of *mu*.

Kenya Hara, the art director of MUJI—a Japanese consumer goods company whose name translates to "no brand" or "no logo"—once wrote that "there is a traditional Japanese aesthetic that sees the utmost richness in what is extremely plain. This plainness is different from the concept of simplicity." While simplicity and *ma* may seem similar, the act of stripping away the unnecessary to achieve simplicity differs from appreciating the substance of emptiness itself. People often focus too much on decluttering when tidying. I was the same way at first. Over the years, I've learned that what matters isn't how much you throw away but how you perceive the space that emerges afterward. Like tidying, the philosophy of *ma* offers a moment to pause and breathe, allowing us to see the spaces we inhabit in a new light.

As I mentioned, *ma* can be found everywhere in Japan.

It goes far beyond aesthetics. It is social. It is ever present in the subtle, abstract interactions of everyday life. It was my children's beloved American nanny who first made me realize how intrinsic *ma* is to a Japanese person. Shortly after our nanny, Lorry, began spending more time with us as a family, she hesitantly brought something up to me.

"I feel kind of anxious when the silence goes on for so long . . ."

At first, I had no idea what she meant, but then I realized she was referring to what she saw as frequent lapses in conversation in our household.

Of course, my husband, Takumi, and I never noticed these quiet moments, as they were a natural part of our daily life. But for Lorry, such *ma* felt uncomfortable, as she instinctively wanted to fill the silence. This was the first time I became conscious of how my Japanese upbringing influenced my comfort with *ma*. Now, when I think back on those times, I smile and feel a bit guilty, imagining how awkward Lorry must have felt sitting in prolonged silence while eating with us or riding in the car.

The Japanese language is famously subtle and indirect. In conversation, we often leave subjects of a sentence unspoken, trusting the other person to infer meaning from context. We pause in silence to reflect on others' words or emotions. When we bow, we take a deliberate pause before lifting our heads, signaling deep respect. We cushion our words gently, always avoiding bluntness. A cornerstone of Japanese social etiquette is the ability to "read between the lines," or *gyokan wo yomu* (行間を読む). You might notice the use of the *kanji* character *ma* (間) again in this phrase. What exactly lies between the lines? Empty space! The ability to see beyond the surface and intuit deeper meaning is the essence of *ma*. Space is limited in Japan, especially in cities like Tokyo. Much like a cluttered closet in need of breathing room, *ma* is a wisdom, developed and refined over centuries, that lets in some light and air through the fabric of society.

After many years living abroad, I've also come to appreciate closeness. The warm encouragement of a handshake or a hug, the art of engaging in lively, intimate conversations. I know that incorporating *ma* into our lives can be challenging—it may feel unnatural at first. Yet I believe, now more than ever, that the world could use a little *ma*. Today, it feels as if every moment and space is filled. Even in the briefest of intervals, our screens are always within reach, filling our senses with noises and information. We're no longer used to sitting in silence, with only our thoughts to entertain us. If you ever feel overwhelmed, I recommend giving yourself some *ma*. You might be surprised how much the breadth of your sensibility can expand.

As my own way of inserting a *ma* into this book, I've intentionally left the next page blank. It contains no words, images, or any other media. It's a pause, a space that exists between this page and whatever you do next. Whether you leave it blank, place a single dot, or fill it with colors is entirely up to you. I hope that this small *ma* brings a touch of harmony and serenity to your day.

Afterword
後書き

As a tidying expert born in Japan, I've had the precious experience of sharing Japanese lifestyle and culture with people around the world for over a decade. Yet, there's something I've become painfully aware of while creating this book: *There's so much about my own country that I didn't know.*

Even for a country where you were born and raised, it can be surprisingly difficult to know its culture and history deeply. But furthering your understanding of a place you're connected to can help you appreciate the richness of the world and give a sense of clarity to your own sense of self. This is very similar to tidying up. What things spark joy for you? What scenery draws your heart?

Afterword

When you truly see the things you like and want to cherish, your world becomes more vivid.

This book covers Japanese history and traditional culture—the Japan as I've seen it through my own experiences. Of course, what's written here doesn't accurately represent everything about Japan. This is because the culture and society of a country can transform every day, and so do its values. Even so, I wanted to capture Japan as I've felt it at this moment in the form of a letter to you.

While working on this book, I was blessed with an invaluable collaborator—Marie Iida, my interpreter and translator who has helped deliver my messages to the world for many years. She has supported me countless times, interpreting during lectures and interviews, and providing English dubbing for my Netflix shows. Her translations go beyond simple word replacement; she conveys my thoughts and backgrounds delicately, moving the hearts of people who understand both Japanese and English. I'm convinced that the existence of "Marie Kondo" that spread throughout the world took shape because of Ms. Iida's support.

Now, I'd like to pause and consider: which aspects of

Japan introduced in this book attracted you the most? Perhaps it was the concept of *wabi-sabi*, hot springs, shrines, food, or the culture of purification? If this book has sparked even one of your interests in Japanese culture, nothing could make me happier.

I also had my own revelations about myself and Japan while writing.

To be honest, I don't perfectly remember the etiquettes I learned in the tea ceremony club during high school. I sometimes hesitated to write about calligraphy, flower arrangement, *aikido*, or even manga—wondering if I had any right to, when true experts already exist.

But perhaps my hesitation itself is quintessentially Japanese.

I'm still not good enough.

It's not perfect, but . . .

The humility, the heart that values respect for those around you—I've become aware of this Japanese sensibility within myself. And today, I have an overwhelming desire to learn about the tea ceremony ritual again. I want to know more about Japanese cuisine and traditional crafts. I want to stroll through a Japanese garden, visit a hot spring I've yet to see.

Afterword

The more I learn, the more I find my curiosity and spirit of adventure to be endless. The Japan that I thought I knew appears before me with a new brilliance.

I'm also thinking about the next generation. My children are growing up and gradually becoming familiar with Japanese culture. In the spring they admire the cherry blossoms, learn about history through manga, clean together at school, and delight at the delicate flavor of *dashi*. They've become accustomed to the buses and trains that run like clockwork, learned to read between the lines and put their hands together in silence at a shrine.

What I wish is for our children to find their own ways to experience the world, to savor diversity, and feel the gifts of culture with their hearts.

Simply put—I love Japan. My own sensibilities as a Japanese person enable me to respect the cultures and values of the many countries I've had the privilege of encountering and feel close to them.

Each new culture I've encountered has amazed me with its own depth and proud heritage.

The quiet dignity that values history.

The sensibility that cherishes art and aesthetics.

Free and open communication.

Each encounter has become an irreplaceable treasure for me.

To respect our differences and to accept them.

It might not be an easy thing to do, but this is how I still wish to live.

Our world isn't perfect. If anything, it's uncertain and incomplete, yet all the more lovable for it. This connects to the concept of *wabi-sabi* that I revisited while writing this book.

How much can we love and accept the world's differences and ambiguities? That may be the very strength required of us in our coming era.

Finally, to my family and team who supported my writing, to Marie Iida who helped create this book together with me, and to the forebears who forged Japanese culture.

For being given the opportunity and role to write this book, I'd like to express a heartfelt gratitude.

Marie Kondo

Note from the Cowriter

An interpreter's job is to bridge a divide. Over the years, as I helped people communicate with each other across languages and cultures, I grew wary of what cannot be translated. I was always hyperfocused on what makes people different from one another. This worldview began to change when I met Marie Kondo.

I still remember meeting Marie for the first time in the early days of her becoming a worldwide phenomenon. At the time, the notable Japanese figures I was interpreting for included professors, artists, and architects, most of whom were older and taller than me, and if I were to be completely honest, they were mostly men.

From the start, Marie had the quiet confidence and grace of someone who knew exactly who she was and what she wanted to do. She dispelled every disadvantage that I always believed came with being a petite Asian woman in a society that insisted we be as loud as possible to be heard. Like me, Marie was born in Japan, and we even shared the same first name. But unlike me, this was her first time living abroad and English wasn't her native language. And yet, here she was, launching a book and a business far away from home.

When Marie invited me to be her on-camera interpreter for her Netflix show, *Tidying Up with Marie Kondo*, I must admit I had my reservations. I worried her methods were a bit esoteric, perhaps a little too Japanese. I was fully prepared for her teachings to be met with confusion or worse. But as we began tidying in the many homes we visited, I heard her clients, sitting alongside her as they folded their clothes into tiny rectangles, nod at her suggestions and say, "I never thought to look at it that way" or "Spark joy. I know exactly what you mean."

The wonderful thing about Marie's tidying method is that it revealed something universal in all of us. We all want to feel more joy in our lives. We want to appreciate what we have. And we all love our homes and wish to take care of them.

In the decade that I've had the privilege of being Marie's interpreter, I've watched her take on everything from speaking at international conferences to presenting at the Emmys. Marie is always quick to give credit to my interpretation, but all interpreters know that we feed off the energy of the person we're interpreting for. If the person is hesitant, then we are hesitant. If the person is courageous and clear-sighted, then we gain the ability to be the same.

Marie might make being joyous seem effortless, but I've learned that it takes dedication to see all the sparks of joy in our imperfect world. I've always thought that Japanese culture was something that my cross-cultural upbringing had deprived me of fully understanding or measuring up to. But in writing this book together with Marie, she has taught me the art of simply appreciating the joys of Japan and opening my heart to what it can teach me.

I believe that Marie's many readers and fans have all taken away different things from the ideas she shares with the world. For some people, it's a tidy sock drawer or a joy-sparking closet. As for me, it's the faith that we have more ways to connect with one another than we might think.

I would like to express my sincerest gratitude to my family and colleagues for their immeasurable support in the writing of this book and to Marie Kondo, whom I'm honored to call a coauthor and a friend.

Marie Iida

Bibliography and References

Kisetsu 季節 **Seasons**

Akihiro Shirai, *Nihon no 72 Kō o Tanoshimu – Kyūreki no Aru Kurashi* (Tōhō Shuppan, Toho Publishing, 2012).

Kawaii かわいい **Cute**

https://japanesekawaiiculture.com

Oshi 推し **Favorite**

Patrick Macias and Tomohiro Machiyama, *Otaku in USA* (Ōta Shuppan, Ohta Publishing, 2006).

Mottainai もったいない

https://zenbird.media/circular-edonomy-japans-successful-circular-economy-400-years-ago/

Chado 茶道 Tea Ceremony

Casa BRUTUS Tokubetsu Henshū Motto Shiranai to Hazukashii! Nihon Kenchiku to Dezain no Kiso Chishiki 2 (Magazine House, 2008).

Noriko Morishita, *Nichi-nichi Kore Kōjitsu – Ocha ga Oshiete Kureta 15 no Shiawase* (Shinchosha, 2008).

Do 道 The Way

Inazō Nitobe, *Bushidō* (Iwanami Shoten, 1938).

Onsen 温泉 Hot Spring

Natsume Soseki, *Botchan* (Sanage Publishing House, 2024), English Kindle edition.

Utsuwa 器 Vessel

Shigeru Uchida, *Futsū no Dezain – Nichijō ni Yadoru Bi no Katachi* (Kōsakusha, 2007).

Onigiri おにぎり Rice Ball

Kana Sugamoto, *Nihon no Omusubi – 47 Todōfuken o Tabi Shite Mitsuketa Mainichi Tanoshimeru Reshipi 94* (Diamond-sha, 2024).

Jinja 神社 Shrine

Momo Kyo, *Kamisama to Kurasu 12-Kagetsu* (Gentōsha, 2024).

Kotoba 言葉 Language

Yōji Hongo, *Jōryū no Nihongo* (Asahi Shimbun Shuppan, 2015).

Katsuyuki Ozaki, *"Arigatō" to Iu Hinsei* (Keibunsha Shobō, 2024).

Koji Takahashi, *Nihon no Yamato Kotoba o Utsukushiku Hanasu – Kokoro ga Tsūjiru Wa no Hyōgen* (Tōhō Shuppan, Toho Publishing, 2014).

Ma 間 Space

Jasper Morrison, Naoto Fukasawa, and Kenya Hara, *Muji* (Rizzoli International Publications, 2010).

Hikaru Suetsu, *Ma no Bigaku – Nihonteki Hyōgen* (Sanseidō, 1991).

About the Authors

Marie Kondo

Marie Kondo is an internationally bestselling author, having sold 14 million books over the last ten years alone, translated into more than 40 languages. She is the founder of KonMari Media, Inc., and oversees the Consultant Program with experts trained in her methods active in over 50 countries. She also hosted the Emmy-nominated Netflix show, *Tidying Up with Marie Kondo*. While globally active, Marie is based in Japan.

Marie began her consultancy as a 19-year-old university student in Tokyo, which inspired her to write *The Life-Changing Magic of Tidying Up*, which landed at #1 on the *New York Times* bestseller list and topped bestseller charts around the world. Marie's simple yet revolutionary approach to living more joyfully has transformed countless homes and lives.

Marie has been featured in *The New York Times*, *Vogue*, *The Wall Street Journal*, *The Times (London)*, and *The Guardian* and on *The Late Show with Stephen Colbert* and *The Ellen Show*. She has also been named one of *Time* magazine's 100 Most Influential People in the world.

Her goal, now and always, is to spark joy everywhere. With *Letter from Japan*, she hopes to share the traditions of her homeland to spark joy all over the world.

Marie Iida

Marie Iida is a writer and Japanese-English interpreter based in Los Angeles. She played a key role as the on-camera interpreter in the Emmy-nominated Netflix series *Tidying Up with Marie Kondo*. Her writing in translation includes over half a dozen monographs on contemporary Japanese artists, including Yayoi Kusama, Toyo Ito, and Kenya Hara for Rizzoli New York. Most recently, she co-translated *Lady Joker* (Soho Press/Baskerville), the acclaimed literary masterpiece by Kaoru Takamura, alongside Allison Markin Powell. She is currently working on her debut novel.